Steve Lehto

The New Lemon Law Bible

Everything the Smart Consumer Needs to Know About Warranty Law

Cover Design: Leah Clark
Cover Photographs: (c) iStockphoto.com (leather) Diane Walters
(lemon) Anna Kucheova

ISBN: 1-4680-4648-9
ISBN-13: 9781468046489

INTRODUCTION

I am an attorney and have practiced Consumer Protection law in Michigan for twenty years. For ten of those years, I taught Consumer Protection at the University of Detroit Mercy School of Law. For several years, I also hosted a call-in radio talk show which dealt with consumer law issues. Over ten years ago, I wrote "The Lemon Law Bible" in an attempt to answer many of the questions I had been hearing over and over again from consumers.

My experience has shown me that consumers are just as unsure of their rights today as ever. Worse, merchants are more unscrupulous than ever before. I decided it was now time for an update of my book.

Although I have tried to include information from every state, I am licensed to practice law in Michigan only. This book is not intended to convey legal advice. It is my goal to allow you to protect yourself in future transactions as well as educate you regarding your current situation. You should still consult an attorney if you have legal needs. If you have a legal problem involving an automobile or other product, I hope this book will help you understand your rights better as well as help you present your case to an attorney.

I will begin with a discussion of the law as it applies to automobiles. Commonly called "Lemon Laws," these are the statutes which protect consumers in all fifty states when they purchase an automobile which turns out to be chronically defective. After that, I will discuss warranties and how they affect consumers who have purchased not just cars, but other products. Along the way, I will try to illustrate some of the more common pitfalls facing consumers and what you can do to protect yourself and your pocketbook.

At the end of this book you will find an appendix. There I have placed excerpts of the lemon laws of all fifty states as well as important sections from the Magnuson-Moss Warranty Act, the Uniform Commercial Code, and a glossary of terminology.

Part I
The Lemon Law

Lemon Law Basics

All states have laws that protect consumers who purchase defective automobiles. These laws are often referred to as "Lemon" laws, even though they are often officially known by other, more technical sounding names, such as the "Arkansas New Motor Vehicle Quality Assurance Act." Generally speaking, lemon laws require manufacturers to buy back or replace defective vehicles if the vehicle has a defect that cannot be repaired within a well-defined number of repair attempts or within a certain time frame.

For the purposes of this discussion it is important to remember that the laws vary widely from state to state. The terms and descriptions given here are to familiarize you with the concepts of the law and to guide you in determining how to look up the lemon law in your state and decide an effective course of action for you. The ideas and concepts presented here are designed to help you understand the law.

What Vehicles are Covered by Lemon Laws?

Many states limit their coverage under the lemon laws to just cars and trucks, while some broadly cover other vehicles, such as motor homes and motorcycles. If you have a defective motor home or motorcycle, the first thing you need to do is find out if your state's lemon law covers them. A listing and brief summary of each state's lemon law can be found In the Appendix to this book. If your state's lemon law does not apply, there is a Federal law called the Magnuson-Moss Warranty Act which covers these vehicles in most cases, and because it is a Federal law, you can use it to your benefit regardless of where in the U.S. you live. In addition, there may be other state laws which protect you if you have bought or leased a defective vehicle. For instance, most states have adopted the Uniform Commercial Code which gives coverage in most settings where a product is sold with a warranty.

Many of the lemon laws require that the vehicle be purchased brand new. However, some states do have lemon laws that cover used cars. Michigan, for instance, does not give coverage for most used cars, except for some rare exceptions. Again, you will need to determine the law in your state.

What Makes a Vehicle a Lemon?

Most lemon laws define a lemon as a new motor vehicle that has a defect or condition that substantially impairs the use or value of the vehicle, and which has not been repaired after a reasonable number of attempts. If the substantial defect still exists or recurs after a reasonable number of repair attempts, the consumer has the right to a refund or a replacement vehicle.

This idea, although apparently quite simple, has several key components which must be examined individually. What is a defect or "condition"? Simply put, it is something that the car does—or fails to do—which is unacceptable to the car buyer. Some defects are quite obvious, such as stalling, failing to start, vibration, or pulling to one side while driving. Although everyone agrees that such cars are "defective," many states recognized that manufacturers attempting to avoid liability might try to claim that several "defects" could lead to the same problem. The manufacturer might argue that if they fixed the fuel injectors on one occasion and on another they replaced the fuel pump, the stalling problem was actually two different "defects."

To combat this, many states inserted the word "condition" into the statute as well so to address this concept. If the car suffers from the same "condition" it is irrelevant what particular "defect" was causing it. This is a very important concept; many dealers and manufacturers tell consumers they have no lemon law case because the parts replaced each repair visit were different, or the repairs were different. That does not matter if the condition complained of was the same!

What is a reasonable amount of time for the repairs to take place? Most states define this with a two-pronged measure: either the number of repair attempts made or number of days in the shop for repair. Michigan's lemon law is a good example, as it is similar to many states' lemon laws in this regard. Michigan law mandates that a reasonable number of repair attempts has elapsed if the manufacturer has had at least four opportunities to fix the defect or condition you are complaining of within the first two years of ownership. Think of it as *four times for the same problem*. This prong addresses those defects which are recurrent in nature, the nagging stalling, no-start, transmission-slipping kind of problems that cause dealers to throw their hands up and say, "We can't fix it!" These are by far the most common cases brought under the lemon law. Under Michigan law, the first of the four attempts must also occur within the first year of ownership.

The other prong in most states is the "days down" test. In most states it is between twenty-five and thirty days. This test is met if the vehicle has spent the given number of days "out of service" or "down" in the repair shop for ANY problems within the first year of ownership. Think of it as *thirty days for any problems*. If the magic number in your state is thirty, the vehicle can be out of service thirty times for one day each, twice for fifteen days, once for thirty days or any combination of days for any combination of problems. It is not uncommon for a brand new car that has suffered a catastrophic failure to literally sit for more than thirty days while the dealer tries to determine how to fix it, or while they wait for parts. In most states, the days are counted as days or parts of days. This means that if the car is dropped off at four o'clock p.m., Monday and picked up at nine o'clock a.m., Tuesday, that counts as two days. Some dealers will try and say that the days are counted as they would be for a car rental, but in most states that is not the case. Certainly consult an attorney before taking the dealer's word for it and be sure to check the Appendix to this book, where the Lemon Laws Around the Nation are listed, with this particular section from each highlighted.

Some states have a third prong which is also important, although less common. In those states, if your vehicle suffers a single failure of a safety related system you may be entitled to relief under the lemon law if the defect is not cured after a single repair attempt. This is to cover those rare occasions when a vehicle has a catastrophic brake or steering failure. The legislatures in those states that have this section recognize that a consumer can lose faith in an automobile which has such a defect, even if it has only been repaired once. Obviously, no one wants to keep driving a car with a safety related defect which occurs more than once. If your car does not qualify under this prong, or your state does not use it, your car may qualify later: you will just have to be very careful driving until that time comes.

It is important to note that a defect must continue or recur after a reasonable number of repair attempts—as discussed above—to qualify as a lemon. Many people become frustrated when their car or truck has been in the shop a couple of times or for a few weeks, but doesn't qualify as a lemon. This is frustrating, but the best advice for such consumers is to be patient. If the car is truly a lemon, the problem will persist. If the problem is fixed, the dealer and manufacturer will have accomplished what the law requires them to do: to fix your car in a reasonable amount of time.

How Serious Must the Defect be to Qualify?

Most states require that the defect or condition complained of impairs the use, safety or value of your vehicle for it to be serious enough to require the manufacturer's replacement or buy-back of your vehicle. But what exactly does it mean to "impair" the use of your vehicle? The laws do not give examples or exactly spell this out, but there are some general guidelines. Obviously, if the car won't start, or won't move because the engine or transmission has failed, the ability to use the vehicle has been impaired. Questions arise on smaller problems, such as noises while driving or water leaks, and those are addressed below.

The lowest threshold of the three choices listed above is probably the "value" aspect. In other words, a defect will affect the value of the vehicle before it affects the use, and safety is really only an issue on very large items and systems like the brakes or airbags. If your vehicle whistles when you drive faster than thirty miles an hour, you may ask yourself if that condition will qualify you for lemon law coverage. The answer can be found by asking yourself a specific question with respect to your automobile. If you were to sell the car to a stranger (or trade it in to a stranger) would they likely offer you less money because of the condition? If the answer to that question is "Yes," then there is a good argument that your vehicle's condition is serious enough, since it impairs the value of your vehicle.

Another guideline to follow—although this is not definitive—is what reaction the dealership's service department had each time you brought it in for repair of the condition? Did they spend warranty money and replace parts? If so, their acknowledgment that the vehicle did, in fact, need repairs goes a long way in showing the severity of your vehicle's defect or condition. However, if the dealership repeatedly wrote your car up as a No Problem Found (or NPF) and never spent any of the manufacturer's warranty money in addressing your concerns, you may have trouble making a case.

Keep in mind that dealers make money on warranty repairs so it is not in their best interest to ignore legitimate problems, especially since in most states the lemon laws do not place any liability for buying the car back on the dealership. Many consumers feel that dealers act in conjunction with the automaker to keep a consumer from pursuing this by not finding problems with the automobile. Although there have been instances where a consumer and a dealership's people have been on bad terms with each other for whatever reason, this is not common. In any event, most manufacturers allow you to take your car to any of their dealers for repair. If you are not being treated well by one dealer, go to another! Of course, if two dealers NPF your car's problems, you may want to rethink pursuing the lemon law for that condition.

Notifying the Manufacturer of the Defective Vehicle

Many states require that you send notification to the manufacturer of the problems you are having with your car and your desire to proceed under the lemon law. This "last chance letter" is designed to put the manufacturer on notice of the problems you are having and provide them with a final repair attempt. Again, this is because it is the manufacturer who will have to buy back or replace your vehicle—not the dealership. Before you send this letter, there is a high probability that no one at the manufacturer has any idea that you are having problems with your car.

You should inquire as to the necessity of such a letter in your state, although it certainly cannot hurt to send one even if it is not required. A sample last chance letter is in the Appendix of this book, and you may tailor it to your situation.

In many states, including Michigan, you may send the last chance letter before you have reached the time frames outlined above, on the theory that the "last chance" will constitute just that: a last chance for the manufacturer, which, if they fail to repair the car, will mean that it meets the lemon law's requirements. That means after the third repair fails, or after the vehicle has been in for repairs for 25 days, you may notify the manufacturer that you are giving them a final attempt to repair your vehicle or you will proceed under the lemon law.

You should send notification of the final opportunity to repair (the "last chance letter") by certified mail, return receipt requested, to the manufacturer's regional office, unless your state's lemon law designates someone else to send it to. Be aware that most states require the manufacturer and not the dealer to answer to you under the lemon law. Many consumers get waylaid by wasting time complaining repeatedly to the dealer where they bought their car. Since the lemon law requires the manufacturer and not the dealer to buy defective cars back, dealers often turn a deaf ear to consumers who complain.

The address to send your last chance letter is usually found in your automobile's Owner's Manual under consumer or customer service. Usually, the section will advise that you first complain to the selling dealer and then it will give an address to which you can write a formal complaint. Send your letter there, certified and return-receipt requested. This extra precaution will only cost you a few dollars and many states require you to send the letter this way to avoid the inevitable claims from manufacturers who say they never received the letter.

Keep copies of any letters you send, as well as a copy of the paperwork from the post office showing that the letter was sent return-receipt requested. This is the best way to document that the manufacturer was notified of a final opportunity to repair.

A Final Repair Attempt

The manufacturer may choose not to use this final opportunity to attempt repair. In fact, a large majority of the last chance letters go unanswered. However, if the manufacturer wants to take you up on the offer, they must notify you within a reasonable amount of time and indicate where you are to take your vehicle for the last repair attempt. What constitutes a "reasonable" time is not defined in many states, including Michigan, where no time frame is given in the law. A week to ten days is probably adequate, although this is something you may wish to speak with an attorney about as well.

If they do not notify you, or if they do and the substantial defect has not been repaired, or has been repaired and recurs, you have the right to demand a refund or replacement under the Lemon Law. If the manufacturer does not comply voluntarily with your demand for relief, you may then seek your remedies under the Lemon Law in court, including replacement of the vehicle, or a refund of the purchase price as described below.

You should be aware that in most states, the manufacturers almost never give consumers what they are entitled to under the lemon law without being sued. Apparently, they sell so many defective cars that their first line of defense is to simply ignore consumers who do not have attorneys representing them. On rare occasions, the manufacturers will buy back defective vehicles without being sued, but they only do this when the consumer is represented by an attorney.

If the manufacturer contacts you and requests the last chance to repair—if one is required in your state—you must give them the opportunity. It probably will not hurt your case. Further, most states require the manufacturer to provide you with a loaner vehicle during the final repair attempt, even if one is not mandated by your warranty coverage. Since they could not repair your car in the previous repair attempts, why would they be able to now? On the other hand, cooperating will help your case as you will be able to say truthfully that you attempted to help the manufacturer to resolve your warranty problems. Also, this repair will not cost you anything since most states require the manufacturer to perform the last chance repair at no cost to you, even if your warranty has expired.

What You Are Entitled to Under the Lemon Law

If your vehicle qualifies as a lemon, the manufacturer must either replace your defective vehicle with a suitable replacement of equal value, or refund your money and take the vehicle back. Usually, you may reject a replacement vehicle and demand a refund if you are not comfortable trading your defective vehicle for another made by the same manufacturer. This choice is often the subject of much confusion. The options will be discussed in turn.

A replacement of equal value is a simple concept in theory which often becomes difficult to accomplish in practice. If you are willing to accept another vehicle from the same manufacturer, you can opt for one that is of equal value to the one you have now. In its simplest scenario, imagine that you paid cash for your car and it will be replaced. If the same make and model are available, then the manufacturer will take back the defective car, you'll sign the title over to them and they will deliver another car of the same value to you. Problems can arise from some common occurrences.

First, you may not be able to replace your car with an identical model. This is often the case if the model year has changed. If you bought a 2009 model and the company is building 2010 model-year cars, you may not be able to find a 2009 anymore. Although you can certainly trade into a 2010, the price of the 2010 is likely to be higher than the 2009. This would result in an upgrade charge, which some consumers do not wish to pay.

Most lemon laws allow for the consumer to get a replacement vehicle of a different price than the defective model, but with the understanding that they will have to pay to upgrade if the replacement vehicle is worth more than the original vehicle. Likewise, if they choose a less expensive model as a replacement, they are entitled to a refund. This is something most car companies will accommodate. However, keep in mind that the fairest way to measure the difference in value between two cars is by measuring the difference between dealer invoices, not sticker prices or what you paid for your car versus sticker price.

Many consumers get a large discount from the sticker price when they buy their cars and thus assume that this entitles them to more credit on the vehicle they are trading in or that they shouldn't be charged "full price" for the replacement. Since there is no way to calculate how much you would have been able to talk the salesman down on the replacement vehicle, some fixed number is the only fair basis for calculation. Suggested retail price is the higher of the numbers available to use, although most manufacturers agree to go from the difference between dealer invoice prices. These are the actual prices, more or less, that the dealer pays for the car wholesale. Since there is no haggling on that price, it is the fairest way to compare prices of two different vehicles.

Even if you financed the transaction, you will be able to get a replacement vehicle through what is called a "collateral exchange." Most lemon laws require the banks or finance institutions that loaned the money on the purchase to cooperate in settling these cases by allowing you to switch vehicles on the loan. In essence, if you found a vehicle of the exact same value, your financier would have to allow you to take possession of that car, put its VIN on the loan documents so that it became the collateral on the old loan, and continue making payments on the old loan as if you had this car all along. That way, the down payment and the payments you made will be credited toward the new car, putting you back at square one, but with the new car instead of the old on the loan.

You are not required, in most cases, to trade only for the same model as the one which you are claiming is a lemon. You are generally only required to trade for a vehicle of the same value from that manufacturer. So, if the manufacturer makes another vehicle you'd rather have, and they cost the same, or you are willing to pay the difference, there should be no problem trading into that model. Some consumers seek to trade into models made by different divisions of the same parent manufacturer. For instance, a person with a defective Chevrolet may want to trade it for a Pontiac. Although the manufacturer could do such a trade if they wished, most manufacturers do not like to do these trades across "divisions." Further, most state laws do not require them to. Good advice for people seeking such trades is that they should instead consider the buyback discussed below and take the refunded money and buy the other vehicle. As you can imagine with the various mergers in the automobile industry, trading across divisions, if the law required it, could become confusing. A person with a defective Dodge Viper could have demanded a trade into a Daimler vehicle of equal value.

If you are unhappy with the replacement concept, or if the math doesn't seem to make sense to you, you will almost always have the option of demanding a repurchase—sometimes called a "buyback." This is where the manufacturer buys the vehicle back from you for what you paid for it, less a mileage offset which is discussed under "Reasonable Allowance for Use." The simplest way of looking at it is if you paid cash for the vehicle. The manufacturer will refund you the cash you paid, including a refund of the taxes and registration fees in most states. Other than the mileage offset, this will make you whole financially.

If you chose to finance your vehicle, this will not be a hindrance to the buyback of your lemon car, although it may add a little more confusion to the mix. This will involve the manufacturer paying off the loan, refunding your money and then you surrendering the vehicle to the manufacturer. The refund to you should include all of the money you paid into the vehicle or that came from your pocket including any trade-in value you may have had. However, the refund will have a mileage offset deducted from it. You will not be refunded rebates since they did not come out of your pocket.

Reasonable Allowance for Use—Mileage "Offsets"

Under most lemon laws a reasonable allowance for use will be taken by the manufacturer. This deduction is not much and varies from state to state. Some states measure it by a given amount per mile driven on the vehicle for the time you drove your car trouble-free. This mileage "to the first complaint" is often only $.10 (ten cents) per mile or some other nominal sum. Many states, Michigan included, have recently changed over to a mileage offset which is usually a little more costly for the consumer. It uses a formula which prorates the value of the car over a hundred thousand miles. The theory behind this is that the automobile would be devalued one hundred percent at a hundred thousand miles. Whether or not this is true is irrelevant. The formula is quite often the law.

If this is the formula used in your state, your offset will be calculated as follows: You take the number of miles you drove the vehicle before the first reported complaint—the first time you brought it in for repair for the complained of problem—and make a fraction where you place that number over 100,000. You multiply that by your purchase price and that becomes the mileage offset in the states that use such a formula. Don't let the math throw you; it's not as complicated as it sounds. For example, if you bought a twenty thousand dollar car and drove it ten thousand miles before the first complaint, you would pay two thousand dollars for the offset. This would be derived by placing the ten thousand over the one hundred thousand—which equals one tenth—and multiplying that by the purchase price. One tenth of twenty thousand is two thousand.

Or, the offset = purchase price X mileage at first complaint/100,000. In the previous example, it looks like this: $20,000 X 10,000/100,000 = $2,000.

Some states will also penalize consumers who drove their vehicles more than an average amount, say, more than 25,000 in the first two years. Those states may charge an amount per mile for the excess mileage or may also ask that you calculate the value of those miles the same way you calculate the offset for the miles before the first complaint. In Michigan, the miles over 25,000 are added to the miles at the first complaint and that number makes the top half of the fraction mentioned above. The statute does say that if the consumer can ask the court to waive the excess miles under some circumstances. That would probably require a showing that the miles were incurred in a car that was uncomfortable to drive—one with excessive water leaks for example—or a car that was unpredictable and undependable.

Some consumers question why they must pay anything for the use of the defective vehicle. Although this sentiment is understandable considering the frustration that the consumer feels, the offset for mileage is the only cost to the consumer for the use of the vehicle for the entire time that the consumer drove the automobile. It is not uncommon for a consumer to pay less than a thousand dollars for the mileage offset after using the vehicle for almost a year. This amounts to a monthly rental of less than a hundred dollars. Looked at that way, this a great bargain for the consumer, and certainly offsets much of the trouble and frustration experienced by the consumer.

Reimbursement for Other Costs

Along with the refund of your purchase price under the lemon law, you will most likely be able to get a refund for some other things. These may include costs for repairs that should have been covered by warranty, unreimbursed towing or rental charges resulting from the defect, the unused portion of an extended warranty, unused portion of credit insurance, and other defect-related incidental costs. These costs are important, considering that they either naturally flowed from the defective nature of the car or because they bought you things you no longer need once the car has been bought back.

There are some items that you will not be able to recover, and it is important to keep these in mind. For instance, the insurance you bought for the vehicle itself is not recoverable in most states since it would have been required even if the car had not been defective. Fuel costs are likewise not recoverable. Some items fall into a grey area which the consumer may wish to fight over. If an automobile had a severe pulling condition that caused it to destroy several sets of tires before it was bought back under the lemon law for its pulling condition, then the cost of those tires may be recoverable. Many such items and situations will vary on a case by case basis, but the rule of thumb is that *costs associated with the defects are recoverable; those that are incidental to car ownership are not.*

Finally, there is the issue of aftermarket items added to the vehicle by the consumer. You have the right to remove them if they were not delivered with the car—and their cost wasn't part of the purchase price—and if you can remove them without damaging the vehicle. These items may include an aftermarket sound system or a bedliner in a pickup truck. Some items may not be easily removed, such as running boards or alarm systems, since removing them could leave exposed holes where screws or bolts used to be.

In these cases, you or your attorney may be able to negotiate with the manufacturer to reimburse you the value of these items. After all, they increase the value of the automobile allowing the manufacturer to recover more for the vehicle when they take it to auction. Manufacturers handle the repurchase of aftermarket add-ons differently, but it is generally considered fair if the manufacturer will reimburse you for half the cost of add-ons that cannot be removed. You should be prepared to document the cost of these items by providing copies of receipts proving their purchase price and showing installation charges, if any.

Arbitration

Arbitration is available from most manufacturers if you believe that your vehicle is a lemon or if you are not satisfied with the warranty service you have been receiving. In arbitration, the consumer and the manufacturer present evidence about the condition of the vehicle to a panel of arbitrators. These arbitrators can usually order further repair attempts, partial refunds or full ones. The manufacturers are often bound by the decisions of their arbitration programs, even if the consumer is not. If this is the case, there may be some value in going through such an arbitration. If you are dissatisfied with the results of one of these manufacturer-sponsored arbitrations whose findings are not binding on you, you may then proceed to file suit in a court of law.

The fairness of the arbitration program and the chance that a consumer will be made whole by such a program vary wildly depending on what state you are in and what manufacturer you are dealing with. Some manufacturers run their own arbitration programs, inventing their own rules, choosing their own arbitrators and virtually guaranteeing that the consumer receives a poor decision. It is not uncommon to find that the arbitrator assigned to your case is a retired executive from the manufacturer you are making your claim against. As you may imagine, if such a program is binding on the consumer, it is virtually useless for the consumer to participate in it. Any consumer considering a lemon law claim should consult a local attorney versed in the lemon law to determine what the requirements are in their state with respect to arbitration.

For example, in Michigan as of this writing, none of the arbitration programs are mandatory or binding on the consumer. Nationally, non-binding programs are almost always available, even in states where the arbitration is not required. For instance, all of the Big Three automakers offer some form of non-binding arbitration for consumers. These programs are designed to offer the consumer a last chance at settling their case without litigation.

However, since the programs are usually designed and run by the manufacturers, they often amount to nothing more than a stalling device of the manufacturer. Very seldom, if ever, has a non-binding arbitration program given substantial relief to consumers. At least, that is the case in Michigan, home of the Big Three. If you can afford to waste time, there is no harm in participating in a non-binding arbitration if it is available in your state. Perhaps it is better put: these programs are nothing more than a waste of your time.

For specific information on your manufacturer's arbitration program look in the warranty booklet that came with your car. It should direct you as to how you can get more information on the arbitration program; it may even tell you whether its program is binding on you, the manufacturer, or both. However, the warranty booklet's descriptions of arbitration are often confusing and misleading since the Owner's Manual is usually designed to be sold in all fifty states and the information for all fifty states would be too cumbersome to be included in all manuals. Because of that, the manuals usually include summaries or merely direct you to call a number for more information.

What if I Want to Arbitrate?

Although arbitration is quite often a futile endeavor, some people like to exhaust all possibilities before pursuing legal remedies. If you choose to arbitrate, first determine what legal rights, if any, you are giving up by going through the process. Some arbitration programs are binding on the consumer, the manufacturer, or both. If the program is binding on the consumer, you must realize that you will not get a second chance; whatever you get from the arbitration process, if anything, is all you will get. You will not be able to come back later and raise any further claims, or even claim that the process was unfair. As noted above, some manufacturers who run their own "arbitrations" staff them with their own employees or former employees. When you find yourself letting the former executive of the manufacturer you are complaining about decide your case, you will probably want to rethink your decision.

You are well advised to consult an attorney before committing to arbitration to make sure that the legal ramifications are clear to you. If you are arbitrating, ask the organization that runs the arbitration program to provide you with a copy of the rule book governing the arbitration procedure. As noted earlier, some of the programs have unusual rules that favor the manufacturers and some of the "independent" arbitration forums let the manufacturers write their own rules. As you can imagine, letting one party to a contest draft the rules of the contest can influence the outcome. Further, find out if the procedure requires you to file a claim form to begin the process. If so, you will need a copy of the claim form as well. They will often provide you with a copy of the rules along with your claim form, but if they do not be sure to receive and review the rules before submitting your claim. Otherwise, you may bind yourself to a program or rules you do not even know about.

Whether or not the procedure allows you to submit a written version of your case and argument, you should outline your case briefly. This will aid you in presenting your case at the arbitration hearing, and if you are allowed to submit it to the arbitrators you should do so. It is very important that you draw up this outline carefully and follow some simple guidelines.

Keep in mind that the hearing is to determine whether your car qualifies under the lemon law, or to see if the warranty on your car has been breached. Therefore, you should keep your presentation to a simple review of the pertinent facts: 1) the purchase information (date of purchase, sales price and whether the vehicle was "new"); and, 2) the repair history. Beyond that, anything you add to the story will probably obscure or muddle your case and not help you. Avoid adding extraneous narrative to your presentation, no matter how tempted you are. For instance, do not bother telling the arbitrator about the problems you have had with the service personnel at the dealership. Those facts, even though they may upset you, do not have any bearing whatsoever on your lemon law case.

The purchase information should *only* include the date of purchase, whether the car was new or used, and how much you paid for the car. That's it. You do not need to go into whether the car was sold at a good price or not, whether it was ready for delivery when they promised you, or whether it came with a full tank of gas or not.

The repair history can read like a time line or a list, showing the dates of the repairs, the mileage at those repair visits, and what the primary complaint was. Avoid giving lengthy descriptions of everything you complained of. If the primary problem with your car is engine hesitation, and you have five documented repair visits for it, do not bother listing other unrelated items which may have been addressed as well. Doing so waters down your case and may make you look nitpicky or overly sensitive. Then, attach good high quality photocopies of the purchase documents and the repair orders to your time line. Make extra sets of copies of this package, so that you have one in your hand and each arbitrator has their own copy.

A consumer is wise to approach arbitration with caution. One consumer whose car's engine exploded within ten thousand miles of purchase was shocked to discover that arbitration denied finding any defect with her car. When she got the ruling from the arbitrators it actually said that the car had been undriveable—it was since it had a blown engine—and therefore the arbitrators were "unable to confirm" her complaint of an engine failure. The arbitrators denied her claim. Luckily for her that arbitration was not binding. If it had been, she would have been stuck with the defective car; instead her lemon law attorneys persuaded the manufacturer to repurchase shortly after she sought legal help.

Stories like these from warped arbitration hearings are legion. At one where the manufacturer agreed with the consumer that his vehicle should be bought back, the sides agreed to simply ask the arbitrator to determine the mileage offset. The consumer had brought his car in at 5,000 miles for a problem that may or may not have been the same one he complained about at 10,000 and then beyond. The parties agreed that the arbitrator was simply to pick which mileage offset to use. The arbitrator—a retired executive from the manufacturer—determined that neither date mattered. He found the vehicle was not defective and did not qualify under the lemon law at all. This, after the representative from the manufacturer conceded the vehicle was not repairable, it was a lemon, and the manufacturer was willing to buy it back.

Recovery and Payment of Attorney's Fees and Litigation Costs

Most state lemon laws allow you to recover your attorney's fees from the manufacturer if you are forced to litigate your claim. This means that an attorney experienced in these laws should be willing to take your case and charge you little or no money for fees. He or she will be able to recover them from the car maker. This fee-shifting aspect of the law is very important because it levels the playing field for consumers. Otherwise, consumers would be forced to fund their own costly litigation while they are also struggling to get by with a defective automobile.

While examining your options when pursuing a lemon law claim, be sure to not only inquire about the expertise and experience of the attorney, also ask whether you will be required to pay any of the attorney's fees before the case is settled. Keep in mind that in many states attorneys are required by law to have the consumer pay the out-of-pocket costs of litigation such as filing fees and court costs. The attorney's fees are often the major expense of litigation. You should always shop around and see if you can find a qualified attorney who will commit to taking your case without asking you to pay any attorney's fees before the case is resolved.

How Do I Find the Best Attorney to Handle My Lemon Law Claim?

As with any other decision you make, you should weigh all of your choices carefully before picking an attorney to handle your case. In most states there are several attorneys who specialize in automobile warranty law. Good sources to locate them include the Internet, local bar associations, yellow pages and referrals.

If you go to an Internet search engine and run a search of "lemon law" and your state, you should turn up a few attorneys who handle these claims. You may also search attorney sites on the Internet, such as which categorizes attorneys by specialty and region of practice. For instance, if you live in Michigan and are looking for a lemon law attorney, you can enter those two specifications and get a list of several choices. Ralph Nader's organization, the Center for Auto Safety, also maintains lists of lemon law attorneys around the country. They can be found at

Likewise, your local bar association may maintain a list of attorneys who handle specific claims, including lemon law. Try calling the bar association for your city, if you live in a large one, or your county or state.

Cconsider calling any attorney you know, or just one from the phone book and ask them for a referral. Most attorneys know of other attorneys in their region who practice in other legal areas.

However, you cannot assume that because an attorney advertises that he or she handles these cases that they are the best choice for you. You should ask several questions when you contact each attorney and compare their answers before making a choice.

First ask how long they have been handling lemon law claims. Although the ones who have the longest tenure in the field are not automatically who you should go with, you would rather have someone with five years of experience than someone who has only one year, and so on. This is only one consideration, though. What percentage of the prospective attorney's practice is lemon law? There are some attorneys who do nothing but lemon law, who probably should be favored in your decision-making process over those who only dabble in the field.

Ask how many lemon law claims they have handled. Dozens, hundreds, thousands? Believe it or not, specialists in this field who have practiced more than a few years can tell you truthfully that they have handled thousands of these claims.

These are the kinds of attorneys you want; they will prove more competent and efficient, saving you time and increasing the prospect of a good settlement on your behalf.

Finally, you should ask how much money the attorney requires up front and who is responsible for paying the attorney's fees. Obviously, if you can find an attorney who requires no money up front and will never require you to pay fees, win-or-lose, is a better choice than an attorney who wants hundreds of dollars up front and wants to bill you for their services during the case.

Can I Sue in Small Claims Court Without an Attorney?

Almost anyone with a valid claim against another person can file a claim in small claims court in their state. However, small claims court usually severely restricts the amount of damages you can claim and what relief you are entitled to. Many states, for instance, cap the amount you can demand in small claims court to $5,000 or less. Lemon law claims are much more valuable, since the cost of an average automobile is more than $25,000.

Further, most small claims courts do not allow you to ask for equitable relief. Equitable relief is when you ask the court to order a defendant to do something. A lemon law claim usually contains a component where the consumer is asking the court to order the manufacturer to buy back the automobile or trade it for a new one. This action is equitable in nature since it is not merely the payment of money. Therefore, these claims are generally not well-suited for small claims court.

Can I Sue in Regular Court Without an Attorney?

Yes, but you wouldn't want to and don't need to. There is no law that says you have to hire an attorney to represent you in any of your legal dealings. People file lawsuits all the time on their own behalf, although successful outcomes in these cases are quite rare. There are two major considerations you need to think about. The first is that the manufacturer has hundreds of attorneys at its disposal, quite likely they are even on the payroll of the automaker. This means that the full legal resources of one of the largest corporations in the world will be pitted against you.

If you have no legal training, the manufacturer will realize that very quickly and try to take advantage of the disparate positions. They will file endless documents, requests, motions, and such to see if you can keep up with them without making a mistake. The courts do not have to give you special treatment when you are representing yourself; in fact, many judges dislike people who come into their courtrooms without attorneys. Corporate defense attorneys routinely get these cases dismissed because a plaintiff with no attorney may have failed to file the proper document on time or may not have seen the importance of something filed by the defendant until it was too late.

Second, you do not gain anything by representing yourself if you have a valid lemon law claim. This is because most states' lemon laws allow for the attorney to recoup his fees from the manufacturer if the claim is successful. The automaker will have to pay your attorney on your behalf under these laws. Why not hire an attorney when, in effect, he or she is being paid for by the automaker that built and sold you a defective automobile?

Beware!

Automakers often approach consumers who own lemon autos and attempt to mislead them into either thinking they have no case or into settling for less than they deserve. Consumers regularly tell lawyers that the automaker's representative told him or her that there is no lemon law in their state, or that their car doesn't qualify when it does. As you can imagine, the automaker has no incentive to tell the truth in such a setting and gains an advantage by confusing or misleading the consumer. If you speak with someone from the automaker, remember that they gain nothing by telling you the truth and it is in their best interest to convince you that you have no case. Do not take their word for it. Study your situation in light of everything you have just read.

Likewise, many times, the automaker will approach the consumer and offer to "resolve" or "settle" their lemon law case. This offer is often followed by another offer which does not give the consumer anything near what they deserve. Most common is the offer to "trade" the consumer into a "replacement" vehicle where the consumer is only credited for the blue book value of the lemon vehicle rather than the full purchase price, as mandated by most state laws. Never accept a settlement offer from a manufacturer until you have consulted with an attorney. Most attorneys will review a settlement offer like that at no charge. Call around until you find an attorney who will review the settlement offer for free.

Many consumers also call the toll-free numbers in their owner's manual and file a complaint with the manufacturer, thinking that this will accomplish something. It won't. The manufacturers have call centers that take these calls, record them, and then do nothing with your complaint. They may even go so far as to give you a "claim" or "file" number. Yet, I have never heard of a consumer—in 20 years—getting a call back from a manufacturer's call center. I've also never heard of the call center doing anything more than giving the caller a claim or file number. I can tell you that I have had this backfire on consumers. The call centers record the phone calls and if you say anything that might hurt your case, they will pull it out later and use it against you. Express too much frustration when you call and they will try and portray you as unbalanced.

Is My Demo Covered by the Lemon Law?

When you buy a car, it is usually designated "new" or "used." Some states allow a seller to also call a car a "Demo" at the time of sale, as if the car had been used as a demonstrator model by the selling dealer. These cars have a few more miles than the typical new car, but usually come with a new car warranty. Also, some used cars come with the remaining new car warranty as well, even though they are used. In some states, these cars may qualify as "New."

In Michigan, for example, the lemon law defines a New car as any car with a manufacturer's warranty. You could be the second or third owner of a late model car, having bought it used, and the law considers it new under the lemon law. Be sure to consult a local attorney to determine if your used car or demo is considered new. Having overcome the hurdle of newness, however, does not resolve all of your issues. The law in many of these cases measures the time frames for the defects to occur from the time of delivery to the first owner. Therefore, if you bought a car in one of these states a year after it was delivered to the first owner, it is unlikely you would be able to successfully raise a lemon law claim for defects that occurred during your ownership, since those problems arose outside of the vehicle's first year of ownership.

Still, a demo may qualify if the vehicle is delivered to you within its first year of ownership. In these cases, you may want to see if you are the first titled owner. If you are, there is a strong argument that the year of ownership runs from the time you took delivery. It may also, however, run from the vehicle's "in-service" date. That is, the date that the dealership put the vehicle on the road. If you are going to buy a demo, be sure to ask if the vehicle has been titled before and if so, to whom. If not previously titled, ask if the vehicle has been put "in-service" and if so, what the in-service date was.

As a technical matter, you should know that all vehicles in the U.S. leave the factory with a "Certificate of Origin." This document is like the car's birth certificate. It shows the vehicle's VIN as well as its place of manufacture and that the vehicle has not been titled to an individual yet. A certificate of origin looks similar to a vehicle title, but is different enough in appearance for the layperson to spot the difference. If you are buying a car that the dealer says has never been titled before, be sure to ask to see the certificate of origin. If they don't have one, they can't legally sell you the car, so they should have no problem showing it to you.

Some states have unusual laws which consumers would never guess existed. For example in Michigan, used car dealers can buy rental cars at auctions and sell them as "demo" cars. Why? Because their lobbyists talked the Michigan legislature into re-defining "demo" to include former rental cars. So, you know what you think "demo" means and the dealership knows that what they're selling you is a former rental car. Are you being misled? Yes. Can you do anything about it? Probably not.

Will I Have to File a Lawsuit to Use the Lemon Law?

Although the preceding section addressed litigation and some of its ramifications, your attorney may not have to file a lawsuit to get you relief under the lemon law. Most automakers have programs where they accept demands from attorneys on behalf of consumers with lemon law claims. These programs, although not available from every car company, usually offer the consumer complete relief faster than through litigation. The automakers using these pre-litigation processes do so because it saves them quite a bit in the way of legal fees. Defending a case they are probably going to lose is more costly than assessing the case early and resolving it if it has merit. Be sure to ask your attorney whether the manufacturer of your vehicle has such a program and if he or she has used it before and if he or she intends to use it in your case.

You can still expect full relief under a pre-litigation program if your manufacturer has one, since they know that if you are not taken care of you will likely file suit. In these programs, the manufacturer will still pay your attorney's fees. At this point your attorney will have spent less time on the case than if a lawsuit had been filed, thus saving the manufacturer even more money.

Unfortunately, none of the manufacturers allow consumers to pursue this course of action without an attorney. This is probably because the savings gained from settling valid claims swiftly would be outweighed by having to sort through the countless claims which would flood the programs if they were opened up to everyone who was unhappy with the service they received on their car.

Even so, not all valid claims submitted to these early resolution programs result in the manufacturers making worthwhile offers which are acceptable to the consumer. In those cases, the consumer is free to pursue litigation.

What Can I Expect in Litigation?

Litigation is the process of bringing a lawsuit through the court system, ending in either settlement, dismissal, or a trial where the Plaintiff—the person who brought the action—either wins or loses in front of a jury or a judge. The concept of litigation is far too complex to be addressed in complete detail here, but a brief summary allowing you to understand the process more clearly follows.

A lawsuit is commenced by the filing of a Complaint. The Complaint is a legal document drafted by the Plaintiff's attorney, detailing the facts and legal principles under which the Plaintiff claims that the Defendant owes Damages to the Plaintiff. Damages are usually used to describe the harm done to the Plaintiff by the acts of Defendant, and are usually reduced to a dollar figure. Some states allow a Plaintiff to spell out an exact number that they are seeking; other states merely require the Plaintiff to define a range of damages sought. For instance, the Plaintiff may seek damages "in excess of $25,000." A complaint may also seek Equitable relief, where the Plaintiff asks the court to order the Defendant to do something that will remedy the wrong other than pay money damages. In a lemon law case, the Plaintiff often requests that the manufacturer replace the subject vehicle, or that the selling dealer accept its return and refund its sale price.

A Complaint often spells out its allegations in tedious, seemingly repetitive, numbered paragraphs. The style of the complaints vary from state to state, but to most laypeople, they are the height of legalese. Do not be overly concerned if the

Complaint does not make much sense to you. If you review the Complaint filed in your case, just check the dates and facts which are familiar to you and make sure they are correct. The facts of the purchase and repair history, for instance, probably will be prominent someplace early in the Complaint.

The Defendant—the person or company being sued—will file an Answer to the Complaint and usually denies all the allegations in your Complaint, except for the most basic. Some consumers are upset upon discovering this, not knowing that it is standard practice in all litigation. Other than the names of the parties, few litigants will admit to the facts presented by the opposing party's allegations. Many states allow a Defendant four weeks or more to answer a Complaint, and this is a taste of the lengthy time frames to follow. Litigation is not a fast process, and this is one of the reasons that pre-litigation is advisable if available.

Most states allow a period of discovery in cases such as these where the parties are allowed to request and examine the other party's evidence before going to trial. This allows a party with a strong position to try and convince the other side that the case should be settled early. Often this is the case with automakers who do not use pre-litigation. They know that if the case is indefensible, they will try and settle their case early before they incur costly litigation expenses, including the cost of their attorneys.

You should be aware that there are car companies that vigorously defend all claims against them regardless of how futile the defense is. An experienced lemon law attorney should be able to tell you prior to filing suit if this is a possibility in your case. It does not mean that you will lose; it merely means that the automaker, for whatever reason, has chosen as a policy to make the litigation process lengthy, probably to discourage consumers from pursuing their rights.

The period of discovery can run anywhere from a month or two to a year, although shorter periods of discovery are more common in these cases than not, because most judges discourage lengthy discovery where the issues are actually very narrow. In these cases the questions to be resolved by the court are quite elementary: is the car still defective? How many times was it repaired? How many days did it spend being repaired? Judges know these questions do not take a year of discovery to answer. An attorney can request that a case's discovery be fast-tracked in most states and absent a good excuse form the Defendant, most judges will grant it if it is available.

Your attorney will probably have to file a witness list with the court, and provide a copy to the other attorneys, telling them who you are likely to call as witnesses in your case if it goes to trial. To help your attorney, you should make a list of the names, addresses and phone numbers of each person you know who knows anything about the automobile, its purchase, and repair history. This should include anyone who was present at the time of the sale, including the salesperson. Also, the names of people who witnessed the problems with the car, or who worked on the car, as well as the service writers and anyone at the dealership familiar with the problems. Even though many of these people will not be called at trial, you should list them in case the need arises. You can always not call someone on your list; it's just that you can't call someone who is not on the list. Better safe than sorry—although in some instances you may be able to call someone as a witness who is not on your list, if you have a good enough reason for not including them.

You may also be required to provide copies of your documents to the opposing side, even though they may have copies of them already. Forget everything you see on television about surprise witnesses and shocking documents introduced at trial. The modern litigation system guarantees that both sides know exactly what they are up against. Again, this is to aid the parties in examining their strengths and weaknesses and settling their cases if the situation calls for it.

Depositions are common in lawsuits that proceed toward trial. This is where you will sit for questioning by the Defendant's attorneys. You will be testifying under oath, even though these usually do not take place anywhere near a court. A court reporter will be present and will record your testimony. Your testimony is then transcribed into a written record called a transcript which can then be used at trial. The Defendant may be able to ask you a wide range of questions about the case as well as about your background to see what kind of witness you make. Sadly, some attorneys choose to take cases to court, not because their case is strong, but because a Plaintiff testifies or speaks poorly. Every attorney has seen a witness who speaks English poorly struggle to explain his or her case to a jury, only to end badly because the jury did not truly understand the case. Although a good attorney can help a Plaintiff explain the case, an opposing attorney skilled at cross-examination can make the same witness look shifty or untruthful, even if it is only a language barrier.

For this reason, it is important that even at a deposition, you do the best job possible. Look and dress professionally, and present your case as clearly and calmly as you can. Of course, follow your attorney's advice explicitly. Your attorney will be present with you during the deposition, so if you have questions about the proceeding you can get them answered at that time.

Interrogatories are also a common discovery device. They take the form of written questions which the parties may send to each other, requiring the opposition to provide answers under oath. Due to the prevalence of word processors and the availability of inexpensive paper, it is not uncommon for large law firms and big manufacturers to attempt to bury a consumer under a pile of interrogatories. Of course, your attorney can counter the paper storm with a volley of his own. This kind of wasteful litigation is not very common in the field of consumer law, even though it does appear occasionally. Do not let the specter of discovery dissuade or discourage you from pursuing your claims. Otherwise anti-consumer forces would win by playing games rather than by addressing the merits of cases.

After discovery ends the court will usually schedule your trial date, and perhaps a settlement conference or two. Settlement conferences are where the court makes the parties sit down and try to resolve the case. As with all the posturing that led to this point, the Defendants cannot force you to take a settlement proposal that you do not like. Although the process can seem intimidating, it is important to remember that the ultimate decision-maker is you, aided by the expertise and counsel of your attorney. Settlement conferences are also sometimes the first time that the consumer is required to set foot in the court. Up to this point, most of the hearings have only required the attendance of the attorneys.

If the case fails to settle, the court will make you come back for trial. The setting of a trial date is often the most frustrating aspect of litigation, both to the parties as well as the attorneys. Most courts' dockets—the lists of untried, pending cases—are overwhelmed. That is, they have a backlog of cases that need to go to trial and not enough time to conduct all the trials. Some courts will merely give you a trial date a few years down the road with the suggestion that perhaps you should settle your case before trial. Other courts will schedule you for trial, along with a dozen or so other pending cases and make all the parties for all the cases show up as if they were going to trial that day. The court will then bring the parties in a pair at a time and try to chide them into settling with the threat that the case will either go to trial today, or may not go to trial for another year, hoping that the uncertainty and strain of gearing up for trial over and over will cause the litigants to settle their claims. Eventually, parties that do not agree to settle their cases get a trial.

A case can be tried either by a judge or by a jury. The choice between the two often must be made at or near the time that the lawsuit is filed, so it is probably something that you will discuss with your attorney before filing suit. Most consumer attorneys agree that lemon law suits are best tried by juries. Jurors are just people taken off the street without special legal knowledge, except for the random attorney who may get called for jury duty, and they can often relate to the problems a consumer encounters when buying a defective car. If your attorney suggests a bench trial, be sure to ask for a clear explanation of his or her rationale. It is possible that the judge you have drawn is favorable to consumers or is known to be anti-big business. An experienced litigator will know who these judges are in each jurisdiction and will use this knowledge to your advantage.

The trial itself is just like those you are familiar with on television and the movies in how they proceed, although in real life they take much longer and move more slowly than you might expect. The attorneys may help selecting the jury and then they will make opening statements. The Plaintiff gets to call witnesses first and the Defendant gets to cross examine those witnesses. After the Plaintiff rests his or her case, the Defendant will call its witnesses, which the Plaintiff gets to cross examine, and so on. After all the witnesses and exhibits have been introduced, the parties make their closing arguments and then the judge reads jury instructions to the jury.

The jury will deliberate and answer questions given to them by the judge. These may be detailed questions such as "Did Defendant breach the warranty?" or be simple, such as "If the Plaintiff is entitled to recover damages, how much?" Many people are confused by the roles of juries versus the role of the judge in a trial, often leading to the question, "Can you appeal if the jury makes a mistake?" Judges rule on the law; juries rule on the facts and how they are applied to the law. Therefore, if the judge makes a mistake in one of his rulings on the record, an appeal may be proper.

For instance, whether a piece of evidence is relevant is a question of law. If the judge admits into evidence something that is irrelevant, that point may be appealed. However, if the jury hears contradictory evidence—one party says a stop light was red, another says it was green—and chooses to believe your opponent's version of the facts, that decision would be difficult to overturn on appeal. Usually, if there is any testimony or evidence at all to support the jury's finding it will be upheld on appeal.

The deliberations of the jury take place behind closed doors and their factual findings are almost never overturned. The main occasions where they are is if they are against the great weight of evidence or if they have reached an impossible verdict, and these standards are usually difficult to reach or prove. Suppose you introduced five repair orders which the Defendant admitted were authentic and evidenced the replacement of a transmission each time. If the jury found specifically that you had not presented your vehicle for four repair attempts, you may be able to appeal that finding on the grounds that the jury reached a finding that went against the great weight of the evidence.

However, the courts of appeal in most states grant juries much deference in examining their verdicts and will not overturn them unless the finding was impossible, no matter how you twisted and turned the evidence. In this example, the Court of Appeal would look at all the testimony surrounding the repair orders and see if there was any way in which the jury could justify its finding. If any such reason was found, no matter how remote, the ruling would most likely be left to stand.

What Happens at the End of a Successful Lemon Law Case?

If you prevail after suit, or you get the manufacturer to agree through settlement to resolve your case, one of several things can happen. If the automaker agrees to repurchase the automobile from you, they will refund what you paid for it in exchange for you returning the car to them. If there is an outstanding loan balance on the vehicle, the manufacturer will pay off the lien to allow you to get a clear title, and pay you back the down payment and the payments made as the refund. You may also be reimbursed to the other items previously discussed.

If you receive a trade—that is the manufacturer is going to replace the defective vehicle with a new one—you will be asked to go and find a suitable replacement vehicle. They will probably direct you to do this at the dealer that sold you the current vehicle. Once you find a suitable replacement, they will make arrangements for you to drop off and sign over the title to the old vehicle, in exchange for delivery of the new automobile. If there is a loan on the old vehicle, they will also arrange for the paperwork on the loan to be rewritten to reflect the exchange of collateral on the note.

In both of these instances the manufacturer will require you to return the vehicle with no damage. You are allowed to have normal wear and tear on the car, but this only amounts to the usual wear that occurs from driving. Cracks in the window glass, for instance, are not normal wear and tear and you will be charged for the repair if you do not have the window fixed before you bring in the car. Cigarette burns in the upholstery and broken trim are also common damage found on cars which the manufacturer will expect the consumer to pay for when relinquishing the car. However, worn tires and faded paint are examples of things that the consumer should not have to pay for.

How Long Should I Wait Before Contacting an Attorney?

It is natural that many consumers want to try everything possible before seeking legal help with their defective automobile. Although this is admirable in most settings, it is not advisable for the consumer to wait once their vehicle qualifies as a lemon. If you think your vehicle qualifies, or if you are not sure, contact a local attorney familiar with the lemon law and find out. Be sure to let them know when you bought or leased the car when you speak with them.

One of the most common refrains heard by consumer law attorneys is, "I never thought I'd ever have to sue someone!" Don't feel bad. The car companies are banking on the fact that some consumers out there will simply live with their defective cars because they feat litigation. Very few people enjoy litigation but it is not something to be ashamed of. If the car companies did the right thing, no one would ever have to sue them. Although our society has attached a stigma to litigation—suggesting that America is "sue-happy" for example—some litigation is necessary. The car companies view litigation as just part of their business operation. The consumer with a defective automobile needs to approach it the same way.

Many people do not realize that if you ignore your legal rights long enough, they will be lost forever. A person who has waived their legal rights cannot ever pursue them, and if for instance, they bought a lemon and did not pursue the claim in a timely fashion, they are stuck with the problems of the lemon. Attorneys in all fields of law tell of potential clients who come to see them with what would otherwise be very worthwhile cases to pursue, only to realize that the person came to them too late. This is because all civil laws, even consumer laws, have statutes of limitation. When these time limitations run out, the case cannot be pursued. These deadlines vary from state to state and even among the laws. For instance, it is not uncommon for some laws to require a plaintiff to file within one year of the claimed wrongdoing; another statute might require the suit to be filed within four years.

It is important that you speak with an attorney as soon as possible when you think you may have a case. This is why we have discussed the possibilities of what may transpire before litigation, with the caveat that delays are bad. Often, dealership, manufacturer, or arbitration personnel will appear to be dragging their feet in responding to your claims. Delays favor the automaker, since they push you closer to the point where the statute of limitation will expire and you will lose your right to bring a case to court altogether.

Part II
Warranties

What is a Warranty?

Warranties and breach of warranty are largely misunderstood areas of law. Warranty protection is something that comes into play in many consumer settings, so you should know about the full coverage of this area of the law. Most of us think only of warranties in the terms of the 3 year/36,000 mile type of warranty that comes with a new car. Of course, the length and terms of these warranties vary between different manufacturers and also whether the warranty is a "bumper to bumper" warranty. Such a warranty covers your powertrain including the engine, drive train, transmission, steering components, suspension, and electrical systems, but does not cover other items, such as "wear" items—like tires.

One of the first areas of concern to the consumer is that the average driver logs more that 12,000 miles per year in their new car, making this "bumper to bumper" warranty inadequate for their needs. To protect one's self, the consumer should have a thorough understanding of what the manufacturer's express warranty will and will not provide.

Basic Warranties

Most manufacturers describe their warranties in terms of the basic warranties and additional warranties or services. The basic warranty should include all repairs and services free of charge, including the cost of labor, for defects in material and workmanship that are discovered during the warranty period. This is an industry wide standard. As you can imagine, a warranty that excludes coverage for labor is really only half a warranty at best, since the labor costs for most repairs exceeds the costs of parts and materials.

The warranty should not require you to perform any duty or act before you are qualified for coverage. Some smaller warranty companies will require consumers to file cumbersome forms before getting coverage, or will require you to take your car to a repair shop of their choice. Most automakers will only require you to take the car to one of their dealers and report the defect. Either of these possibilities is workable, but you should be aware of what you will be required of you before you buy the car and its warranty.

The basic warranty should cover you, the purchaser, and any subsequent owners, until it expires on its own terms. Most factory warranties are transferable to someone you sell your vehicle to, with the buyer assuming the remainder of the warranty coverage. Most factory warranties can be transferred at no cost, although some automakers do require a registration or transfer fee to be paid by the buyer. Some carmakers also exclude coverage for second owners of leased automobiles.

The presence of the transferable warranty is important to you if you are the original purchaser of the car. It will greatly enhance the resale value since many people will offer you less money for a used car if it is not warranted by the manufacturer. Likewise, if you are shopping for a used car, look for one with the remainder of the manufacturer's warranty intact. This extra coverage is often seemingly priceless if the vehicle develops problems down the road.

Things Not Covered by a Bumper to Bumper Warranty

You should realize that "bumper-to-bumper" warranties may often exclude some items from coverage. A bumper to bumper warranty will probably not cover normal wear and tear, maintenance items such as oil changes and tune ups or damage or harm from collision, vandalism, lack of maintenance, improper or abusive use, or natural "acts of God." While these exclusions are reasonable, keep in mind that some dealers and manufacturers try to escape warranty liability by claiming that these exclusions led to the problems in your vehicle and are not the result of a legitimate part failure.

Knowing this, you should always save receipts for oil changes, tune-ups, and any other service you have performed on the vehicle during your ownership. For instance, it is not uncommon for a dealer to claim that an engine failure was caused by a lack of timely oil changes. If you have receipts showing the proper oil changes, they will have to drop this argument. Without such receipts there is a good chance that your warranty coverage will be denied and that you may have to pay the repair costs out of your own pocket.

Although you can probably get service for all warranted items at the selling dealer, not all of the items on a new car are actually warranted by the automaker. Some, such as tires, batteries, or car stereos may be warranted by their manufacturers. Make sure you receive copies of such warranties at the time of purchase, and note what the terms are. Some of them may not be simple repair or replace warranties as you would normally expect. For instance, many car or tire warranties prorate how much credit you will receive for a replacement, perhaps giving you only a discount on the new item if the old one goes bad. Although this is an industry-wide practice, many consumers are surprised to learn this.

Most automakers offer corrosion or body finish warranties. These cover premature rust or paint defects, although some may not cover minor surface problems. Modern car manufacturing procedures allow most car makers to manufacture cars and trucks that will not rust until long after these warranties expire, but you should study the terms available on the vehicle at the time of purchase.

Many dealers will seek to have you buy extra rustproofing or body/paint sealant. Most manufacturers will not recommend such treatment, even though their dealers often sell these items at astronomical mark ups. You should never bother to buy these items as they are unnecessary, and more importantly, some manufacturers will tell you that these processes void the corrosion warranty!

The Express Warranty

The manufacturer's bumper to bumper coverage describes only one kind of express warranty. An express warranty is any statement or promise that the seller makes to you regarding the goods you are buying and their quality or performance. The definition, as found in the Uniform Commercial Code states that express warranties by the seller are created in one of several ways:

The seller makes an "affirmation of fact or promise" to the buyer which relates to the goods and becomes part of the basis of the bargain. In this case, there is an express warranty that the goods shall conform to the affirmation or promise. "If this item breaks down within one year, I will replace it," is a promise that you could enforce later as an express warranty.

A description of the goods which is made part of the basis of the bargain creates an express warranty that the goods shall conform to the description. An example would be that the seller promises to deliver a new television to you but delivers a used one instead. The designation of the set as "new" is a warranty, and you could sue the seller for damages from the breached warranty (along with the other causes of action that would arise from that sale.)

Finally, any sample or model which is made part of the "basis of the bargain" creates an express warranty that the whole of the goods shall conform to the sample or model. This situation arises often in industrial settings where a seller shows the tentative buyer an example of what will be furnished later. The model or sample itself, if held out as what the later delivery will comprise of, is a demonstration of the warranty.

It is not necessary in an express warranty that the seller use formal words such as "warrant" or "guarantee" or that he or she has a specific intention to make a warranty. Simply put, the following advertisement, "1969 Corvette, 20,000 actual miles, first-owner selling," contains several warranties. The year of the car is warranted as 1969; if you bought this car and it turned out to be a 1968, you could sue the seller for breach of warranty, even if the seller believed the car to be a 1969. If the mileage on the odometer was incorrect and you could prove it—say that you found out the odometer had rolled over 100,000 miles—you could likewise sue the seller for breach of warranty and recover your damages if you proved your case. "First owner" is even a warranty.

When making any purchase, pay close attention to the statements the seller makes, whether written or spoken. Those statements may give rise to warranties that you can later rely upon. If warranties such as these are made and broken, you may be able to recover your damages from the seller for Breach of Warranty.

The Limited Warranty

A carmaker may also offer an express limited warranty, reducing the coverage offered to certain parts or systems of the car. For example, some carmakers offer a short bumper to bumper followed by a longer limited powertrain warranty. Many used cars are also sold this way.

The law specifically allows warrantors to limit coverage of their warranties so long as the warranty is clearly labeled "limited" and the limitations are spelled out for the consumer before the purchase is made. Read the warranty booklet for your automobile carefully before you purchase if you have any doubts about the coverage or if the salesperson can't give you satisfactory answers regarding what is covered and what is not.

Service Contracts

Service contracts are different from warranties, even though many people confuse the two because they both provide repairs for your vehicle after you have purchased it. A service contract is a written agreement to repair certain items on your vehicle for a specific period of time or mileage. Service contracts are usually very straight forward but quite often offer less coverage than an express warranty, even a limited one. Because of that, it is very important for you to understand them fully.

Oftentimes, the only functional distinction between a service contract and a warranty is the party obligated by it. Most warranties come from manufacturers; many service contracts come from third-party service contract companies. Some manufacturers offer service contracts but you need to be careful While these are better than the service contracts offered by third parties, they are not as good as warranties offered by manufacturers. I have spoken with numerous consumers who were told that their vehicle was being sold to them with a "warranty," only to find out that what they were getting was a service contract. What is the difference? Here, it was the fact that the service contract contained limitations and offered much less coverage than a typical manufacturer's warranty.

Service contracts are better thought of as contracts rather than as warranties. Many people confuse the two or use the terms interchangeably, even though they are quite different. Simply put, a contract is a legal agreement to perform—in this instance, service or repairs—given in exchange for money. You pay; they repair.

Under the general concept of contract law, parties are allowed to enter into agreements for any legal purpose under any terms that the parties agree to. Service contracts are usually drafted and proposed either by a manufacturer or by a third party service contractor, so there is not much room for negotiation except on price.

However, there is often a choice to be made by the consumer as to the lengths of coverage available. The coverage terms are usually expressed in the same manner as limited warranties: it is not uncommon to find a 12 month/12,000 mile or a 3 year/36,000 mile service contract.

The primary difference with a service contract is that it will be limited to merely repairing items that break on your automobile. The service contractor is not undertaking the obligation of replacing the vehicle if it is irreparable. The mere sale of a service contract with an automobile will not create lemon law liability for the consumer to pursue.

Still, service contracts are much better than no coverage at all. In fact, they are often the only coverage available for used cars, especially older or higher mileage ones. Again, you should shop carefully to see what coverage the service contract provides and see if it is worth the price. Some service contracts cover many items and systems, such as engines and drive trains, while others restrict coverage to just the engine, for instance. Some service contracts—even ones offered by manufacturers—contain silly exclusions. Some, for example, commonly exclude the cost of "hoses" from any repair bill, even as they cover the engine. So, when your engine fails and is repaired under the service contract, the repairing dealer will either have to use all the old hoses on the new engine, or charge you the cost of replacing the hoses. Any mechanic will tell you that the hoses need to be replaced and re-using them would be silly on a new or rebuilt engine. Why do they exclude the cost of the hoses? To save themselves money. There is no other logical reason for doing it.

Some service contracts are transferable, also giving them more value, just as a transferable warranty increases the value of the car or truck you own. You should carefully examine both the terms of the contract—the length of coverage—as well as how those terms are calculated. If a service contract runs 12,000 miles, is that 12,000 from your purchase or from the prior owner's purchase?

Oddly, there are service contracts sold by Big Three automakers which start their coverage from the "in-service" date—that is the day the car was sold to its first purchaser. Although this often causes confusion among consumers, the contracts usually state somewhere what the expiration date and expiration mileage is for that particular contract. Examine these dates carefully and be aware of the limits of coverage as they approach. If your engine is covered and begins to develop a noise, you should take it in for repair before the limits expire, otherwise you will not be able to seek the coverage under the contract.

There is one other aspect to service contract which is important to consumers. The Magnuson-Moss Warranty Act prohibits sellers from disclaiming the implied warranty of merchantability during the term of a service contract. So, in effect, the purchase of a service contract gets you a warranty as well—at least for the length of the contract. With that, you gain all the rights and remedies of warranty law. Most important there is your ability to revoke acceptance of the automobile if it turns out to be severely defective and the service contractor fails to remedy the defect in a timely fashion.

What If I Have Problems After My Warranty Has Expired?

Even though your warranty coverage expires at a specific time or mileage do not give up hope on getting free or discounted repairs from the manufacturer. Almost all automakers offer "goodwill" repairs on vehicles which develop problems outside of warranty, but you have to know how and who to ask to get this coverage.

Generally speaking, if you have a problem that would have been covered by warranty if it had occurred just a little bit earlier, you have a good chance at getting coverage. The longer it is since your warranty expired—in time or miles—the lower your chances become. Since there is no bright line rule on this, however, it is always something you should try before you give up and pay for the repair out of your own pocket. If your vehicle has a defect which occurs outside of warranty, take it to the dealer where you would have taken it during the warranty period, and explain to the service writer that even though your warranty has expired you think the problem should be fixed by the manufacturer. There are several things you should explain to the service writer as well, depending on which of the following actually apply.

First, if this is a repeat of a problem that they have addressed before, point this out to them. That way, it is not really a new repair or problem, it is merely a prior repair that was performed improperly. Next, explain to them that you have always been happy with this dealership and this manufacturer, but you have decided that you are going to switch brands because of this problem and will not buy your next car from this dealership, even though that is what you were planning to do. If the service writer will not commit to giving you a free repair, do not give up. Go over his head and ask to speak to the service manager. Repeat all of the above arguments to him or her. If this fails, ask to speak with the dealership manager. You may also want to enlist the help of your salesperson, since this person is going to lose a commission if you do indeed choose to buy your next car elsewhere.

Finally, ask to speak with the manufacturer's zone manager. Each manufacturer has personnel who travel each region of the country, visiting the dealers in that area, helping them with warranty repairs and acting as liaisons between the dealerships and the automaker. These people have the authority to approve goodwill repairs if the dealer doesn't want to do it. Attorneys who have spoken with zone representatives have been told that customers who politely ask for repairs, even though their warranty has expired, often get goodwill repairs for no other reason than to keep a customer happy.

Dealerships will usually not give you the zone rep's name or number, but will tell you what day he or she will be at the dealership next. Most are happy to pawn you off on the zone rep since it means they can stop dealing with you. When the zone rep is in town, go and see him or her, explain your case as clearly and businesslike as you can and take anything they offer you. Some will offer to split a repair bill if they won't pay for the whole thing. Some will offer free parts if you pay the labor. If they offer you nothing, take your car to be repaired somewhere else.

Dealerships are usually much more expensive than non-dealership repair facilities and their work isn't any better. While you're at it, buy your next car somewhere else.

What Does it Mean to Buy a Vehicle "As-Is"?

Many people wonder what it means to buy a vehicle "as-is". The reason this is such a concern is that a very large percentage of used cars sold in this country are sold "as-is." This includes almost all used vehicles sold by used car lots and those sold by individuals, such as those advertised in your local paper's classified ads. Buying such a car curtails your rights so extensively that if you do not understand what you are doing when you buy a car "as-is" you may suffer serious financial harm.

The law in most states allows car sellers to limit what kinds of warranties they offer to buyers at the time of sale. They can even opt to sell a car or truck without any warranties whatsoever. This kind of sale is often called "as-is" with the vehicle being sold "with all faults." The confusion that arose in this field of law inspired the Federal Trade Commission to get involved and mandate disclosure forms which all used car dealers are required to use when they sell a car. The "Buyer's Guide" is the name of the disclosure form, and it requires the seller to explain which of the following two options describes how the car is being sold: with a warranty or without one. There are two boxes on the face of the form and the dealer is required to check the box which applies. More often than not the "As-is, no warranty" box is checked, and buyers don't realize the implications of this statement.

The fact that an automobile is sold without any warranties whatsoever means that the car, once it is yours, is no longer the responsibility of the dealership no matter what happens after the purchase. The engine could explode as you drive off the lot just minutes after purchase. The transmission could fail on the way home from the dealership. The car could fail to start once you get it home. If the sale was truly "as-is" there is nothing you could do in any of these cases to get the vehicle fixed by the seller.

This fact understandably upsets many car buyers who were unaware of the impact of the "as-is" disclaimer appearing in their paperwork or on the Buyer's Guide in the window of their used car. Adding to the confusion is often a salesperson who makes statements or promises to get the sale. Often these statements conflict with or appear to contradict the "as-is" disclaimer. For instance, many salespeople will tell prospective buyers that the dealership will "stand behind" the sale or that if anything goes wrong with the car the dealership will fix it. These statements are almost impossible to prove and quite likely conflict with the written documents which accompany the sale along with the Buyer's Guide. Most car dealers use standardized purchase orders and forms which contain language stating that the verbal promises and statements of the salesperson are unenforceable unless reduced to writing. Armed with such paperwork—often signed by the consumer at the time of the sale—sellers routinely deny having ever made any such promises.

Further complicating matters is the fact that most states give a legal preference to written statements over verbal ones. This means that if the salesman says one thing and writes another, a court is more likely to accept the written word over the spoken.

This is not meant to say that sellers who lie to induce sales are right, morally or legally. If a buyer could prove that a seller lied to induce them to buy an automobile, they may be able to use that fact to either undo the sale or to force the seller to keep the promise. As noted above, however, proving such a thing is often next to impossible.

Further, the statements of salespeople fall into a class of their own which will be discussed in a moment. Most states recognize that used car selling naturally involves a certain amount of "puffing." That is, statements of a general nature playing up the car and its qualities. "This car runs great," or "This car is a great bargain," are such statements. Most states would not consider these to be the kinds of things you could hold a dealership liable for if they turned out to be wrong. Listen to the salesman's words carefully; if they are subjective in nature, such as opinions, they are probably not something you can rely on. If they are objective in nature, stating facts that can be measured, they might be more than puffing. Statements such as, "This car has a brand new transmission," or "This vehicle was only owned by one other person before we bought it," are factual statements that could be proven or disproven. They are more than puffery.

A true understanding of the implications of "as-is" purchases is something every car buyer should have. Armed with this knowledge, the consumer should always keep the following in mind. Try not to buy a car "as-is" unless it is absolutely economically necessary. If it is necessary to buy such a car, bring a mechanic with you to inspect the car and try to not pay any more for the car than you would if you knew that it might not be drivable the moment you leave the lot with it. Imagine the worst and spend accordingly. Take an especially thorough test drive, taking the vehicle out on a highway to see how it runs at highway speeds and be sure to climb underneath the car and look to see if there is any apparent structural damage. Although you may feel silly crawling around on your hands and knees in the parking lot of the used car dealer, it will be nothing compared to how bad you will feel if you later discover that you missed obvious body damage that was only visible from underneath the car. Very few late model wrecked cars end up in junkyards permanently. Where do you think they go? Many wrecked cars get repaired and sold "as-is" by unscrupulous car dealers.

Even if a car is being offered for sale "as-is" a consumer may be able to buy a warranty or service contract for it. Ask the salesperson if a service contract or warranty is available for the automobile you are looking at. Even if the service contract is for a limited duration it may protect you from incurring major repair expenses, or at least allow you to drive the car for long enough to know that the dealer wasn't concealing any defects from you at the time of purchase. Further, as mentioned above, during the term of the service contract, the seller cannot disclaim the implied warranties. In effect, they cannot sell you a car "as-is" if they also sell you a service contract with the auto.

This does not mean that a merchant or car dealer can defraud a consumer and hide behind an "as-is" sale either. All an "as-is" sale means is the vehicle is sold with all faults and with no warranty of merchantability. If the dealer lied about the year of the car, or rolled the odometer back, or if the car was stolen, the "as-is" sale would not keep you from going after the dealer to take the car back or pay you damages. Unscrupulous dealers will try to sell salvaged vehicles "as-is" without disclosing the salvage history; or, they will mask known problems in the engine through the use of heavy oil and then sell the vehicle "as-is" knowing the engine will fail days after purchase. Again, a buyer could revoke acceptance of these kinds of vehicles because the active misrepresentation or fraud is not waived by the buyer in an "as-is" sale—only the implied warranty of merchantability. Again, to protect yourself in an "as-is" sale, have the car fully inspected by a mechanic AND negotiate a price that is fair considering the cost of repairs that you may have to make to the car immediately after taking possession.

Part III
Consumer Transactions

Understanding the Documents at the Time of Sale

One of the most confusing aspects of an automobile purchase, new or used, is the increasing number of documents which you will be asked to sign, often without reviewing. Any attorney will advise you to first read and understand every document you sign. If you have questions about the documents or do not fully understand them, *ask questions before you sign anything*.

Then make sure you receive copies of all documents you sign at the time of purchase—never accept a salesman's promise to provide them later—and keep them in a safe place. These documents will often define and describe your legal rights; without them it may be difficult for you to enforce your rights. Further, many consumers are unaware of the rights they sign away or the promises they make when signing these documents without reading them. Although you do not have to sign the documents—you can choose to not enter the purchase contract and shop for a car somewhere else—these documents are usually presented on a "take it or leave it" basis. With that in mind, here is a list of some of the more common documents you may see at the time of purchase and what you should know about each.

Purchase Agreement

This document, sometimes called a purchase order, is often the legal contract underlying the purchase of an automobile, truck, boat or recreational vehicle. The terms of the agreement are usually embodied on this one page. These would include the make, model and vehicle identification number of the car, along with the purchase price, rebates provided, possibly the taxes, title and registration fees and whether or not the vehicle is being furnished with a warranty. If there are any important promises made to you by the salesman—such as a promise of a free extended service contract—you must make sure they are described on the purchase agreement. Every attorney has heard from a consumer who claims that the salesman promised to deliver something and then backed out later; because it wasn't included on this form the consumer couldn't prove the promise was ever made in the first place.

Finance Contract

This is also referred to as the retail installment contract and will be the loan document you sign if you borrow money to buy your car. Often this document is provided by the dealer even though it will bind you to make payments to a third party—a bank or a finance company. This document is also probably the longest and most confusing paper you will see at the time of the sale. A Federal "Truth in Lending" law has caused the banking industry to standardize the forms used to loan money in consumer purchases, so if you've seen one of these documents, you will recognize much of what is on its face. Across the top of the form is a row of boxes showing the amount financed, the interest rate, what the purchase price is and how much interest you will pay over the life of the loan. However, the most troubling and overlooked portion of this form is what is on its back. For instance, there the consumer will read for instance what constitutes a default and what will happen if a default on the loan occurs.

This is another area of confusion to consumers. Many people consumers do not realize that most loan contracts allow for the lender to declare them in default if they are even a single day late making a payment. Most assume that since there are grace periods seemingly built into every transaction we are involved in, they must be required by law. The law does not require the lenders to give you a grace period and if the contract does not give one, there isn't one. If the contract states that your payment is due on the first and is late if not received by the tenth of a given month, it will often state elsewhere that if your payment is not received by the tenth, you are in default.

The laws in most states allow a lender to take drastic action when the borrower goes into default on a loan underlying a consumer purchase. Usually, this means that the lender can repossess the vehicle, often without warning or notice. Disputes often arise when consumers claim that they paid their note on time and their vehicle was repossessed anyway. Although mistakes have occurred in the processing of payments, it is more often the case that a consumer paid late and the lender decided to declare a default, even though they had never done so in the past. This practice is also legal. On most of these loan documents is the statement that a lender does not waive—give up—its rights merely by allowing a borrower to slide once in a while in the past.

Before signing a retail installment contract, it is highly recommended that you read not only the important information on the face but also everything on the reverse, paying particularly close attention to the section describing what constitutes a default and what steps the lender can take upon default.

The same is also increasingly true of purchase agreements. Lately, many car and RV dealers have been using more complicated purchase agreements, often placing draconian terms on the reverse side after putting a warning on the document's face saying, "Be sure to read the reverse of this document." On the back will then be language obligating the consumer to arbitrate any claims with the dealership, including claims about the document itself. Sometimes, the purchase agreement will contain language simply stating that the consumer cannot sue the seller for anything. Courts in some states will allow the dealers and sellers to do this, and tell the consumers, "If you didn't like the contract, you shouldn't have signed it."

As you negotiate the purchase of your $200,000 RV, pause before signing the puchase agreement. Tell the salesman you will only buy the RV if he crosses out that language. Watch what happens. (They will refuse to delete the language but will tell you all kinds of things like, "We never enforce that," or, "That's meaningless, it's just boilerplate." Of course, those are all lies.) It just depends on how badly you want that RV.

Application for Title

Most states require that a vehicle be licensed and registered for use at the selling dealer. The dealership is authorized to process documents that would normally be filled out at a state office. In Michigan, the document that the dealership fills out and files with the state is the RD-108, which is a particularly useful document. It contains much of the same information as the purchase agreement and the loan document but in a more efficient format. Here, you will find the name and address of both the buyer and the seller, the identification, make and model of the car, as well as all the financial information. Many consumer attorneys use this document almost exclusively to gather the important information regarding the sale.

The Warranty Booklets

These are usually handed to you by the salesman or are found in the glove box of the vehicle. There have been occasions when consumers have complained of not getting the warranty booklets or owner's manuals for their cars. Under no circumstances should you ever accept delivery of a car without these important documents. They describe your rights and remedies with respect to your warranty coverage, including the length of the warranty, what is and is not covered, and who you direct your complaints to at the manufacturer.

Rebate Documents

If you received a rebate on the purchase of your car, you may have been required to sign something, especially if the rebate was tied to an employee discount. As with anything else you sign at the time of purchase, keep copies of these documents. Many people are surprised to learn that when they agreed to accept a rebate they agreed to give up rights, or agreed to not trade or sell the car for a period of time. Although these kinds of agreements often occur in transactions such as employee purchases, you may be surprised to see what terms are included in the rebate papers. A surprised consumer is frequently an unhappy consumer.

Brochures or Pamphlets

If you receive brochures or pamphlets that describe the car, its accessories or extended service contract, these are also things you should keep. Many consumers, in the rush to get their new car purchase finalized, forget to save copies of the documents describing the "extras" that they have purchased. These could include alarm systems, extra warranties, bed liners, bumper hitches and any number of things. These extra brochures often describe the warranties that these items come with, and sometimes even the operating instructions.

Service Contract Application and the Contract Itself

Sometimes there is a separate application, sometimes there is just a copy of a contract. Either way, examine the documents carefully and make sure that they agree with what the salesman told you. Many people claim that they were told terms different from what were found in the contract, but didn't notice until after they'd left the dealership. Salespeople will later say that these discrepancies are the results of misunderstandings and will most likely not make good on them later.

Credit Life and Disability Application

If you are inclined to buy this coverage, be sure to examine the application carefully and sign it only after you agree with everything on the application. It is not uncommon for salespeople to sell these policies to people who are not eligible—for instance, to a person who is already disabled—and tell the consumer, "Don't worry about it. We'll submit it and see if you're approved." In these cases, the company will often take your premiums until you file a claim and then deny your claim on the basis that you filed a fraudulent application! The net result, of course, is that these companies will keep your premiums if you never file a claim and never pay you if you do.

Further, the credit life and disability insurance is usually sold at grossly inflated prices by the dealers. If you feel you need this kind of coverage, shop around for it. You will usually find that it is available at a greatly reduced rate from your regular insurance salesperson—the one who sells you auto or home insurance.

Many dealerships who fear losing an insurance sale will try and hard-sell the consumer, often claiming that the insurance is required to make the purchase. In most states it is illegal to require such a thing. If the salesman tells you that the insurance is required by the lender, ask to speak with the loan officer who is making the illegal request. Then tell the salesperson that you will acquire the insurance elsewhere.

Again, if you are inclined to purchase the credit life and disability policy, even though it is probably over priced and unnecessary, be sure to get a copy of the policy and read it before buying it. It contains a lot of important information, including the limits on your coverage. For instance, it is not uncommon for a credit life policy to limit its payout to some random amount chosen by the insurer, with no regard for how much your car payment is. This unusual situation could result in you owing several hundred dollars more each month than the policy will pay when you are legitimately disabled and qualified for coverage.

Also, do not let the salesperson fill the form out. Ask to fill it in yourself, since you will be held accountable for the statements on the application, and false statements will be used as ground for denying your claim. It is sometimes even in the salesperson's better interest to make mistakes on the form so that your claim can be denied if you file one. Oftentimes, the credit life insurance is provided by a company owned by the dealership! This means that the dealership wants to see you buy the insurance but never collect benefits. Usually, the forms are a very simple series of Yes/No questions so there should not be a problem with you filling it out yourself.

The Buyer's Guide

This is the Federally mandated form which must be affixed to a window of the car on a used car lot. This is required by Federal law, so you should see these regardless of what state you go car shopping in. The Buyer's Guide explains whether the car is being sold with a warranty, with no warranties—"as-is"—and whether a service contract is available for the vehicle. The Buyer's Guide creates a very conspicuous disclosure, which unfortunately, a lot of consumers do not understand.

Another problem arises because unscrupulous dealers will either not display the Buyer's Guide or will mislead consumers about their true meaning. Attorneys are all too familiar with consumers who truthfully tell of seeing the Buyer's Guide for the first time after the sale has been consummated—or worse—seeing it for the first time during litigation. If you are buying a used car, look for the Buyer's Guide. If it is not attached to the window of the car you are looking at you may want to pass on considering the purchase. After all, the dealer is committing a federal offense by not displaying the Guide. How trustworthy are they?

Likewise, consumers tell of dealers who told them that the car had a warranty and that the Buyer's Guide was merely a formality. "Don't worry about that. If the car breaks down, we'll fix it." If that were true, the "No warranties—AS IS" box wouldn't be checked!

Repair Orders

Along with the purchase documents, these are among the most important papers with respect to your defective automobile. These are the papers that you receive when your car is repaired under warranty at the dealership. Every aspect of this transaction is important, so pay close attention to the following.

Your first exposure to these documents is when you bring your car in for warranty service. Even if your car is not a lemon, or this is the first time you bring it in for service, you should pay close attention to the transaction. When you speak with the service writer, explain to them exactly what your car is doing wrong and make sure they write it down exactly as you tell them. Do not let them write "No crank-No start" for instance, if your car quit running while you were driving on the highway. They may actually try to do this, and tell you that this a term of art for the service technician. Tell them politely to then write what you told them below what they have already written. Refuse to sign the repair order until they write down what you say. If they will not, write it down yourself. You will be surprised at how adamant some service writers are about not putting down what is actually wrong with your automobile. Also make sure that the repair order accurately reflects the day the car is being dropped off for service and the mileage on the vehicle at the time of drop off.

Be sure to take a copy of the write up with you. Some dealers try to get you to leave without a copy of the write up, down-playing the seriousness of the problem. Every attorney in this field has spoken with consumers who say that the vehicle was not "written up" the first few times it was brought in because the dealer wanted to make it seem like the defects were no big problem. Those missing repair orders can seriously impair your ability to prove your lemon law claim because they are often the only concrete evidence you have that your car was even worked on.

When your car is returned to you, be sure to get a completed repair order reflecting what work was performed on your car, as well as the mileage "out"—how many miles are now on the car—and the date that it was picked up. This document will not only help you prove that the vehicle was brought in for repair of the problems listed but will also aid you in calculating how many days your vehicle was in for service. Do not accept the form if it has incorrect dates, the wrong mileage, or does not reflect what work was performed on the car. Some dealers will try and get you to leave without a repair order, telling you that one was not generated or that they will mail it to you. Do not believe either of these statements.

Pay particular attention to the mileage on your car when you drop it off and pick it up. Every attorney in the field has horror stories of customer cars being taken for long drives while in the possession of car dealerships. I've had clients whose cars were driven *thousands* of miles while being "repaired," and others whose cars were wrecked by dealership personnel out joy-riding.

If warranty work was performed on your car, you know paperwork was generated by the dealership. The manufacturer requires copies of the repair orders to process the payment they will make to the dealer reimbursing them for work done on your car. There is no reason for them to mail you the repair order. It has been filled out before the car was given to you. Although it is common to hear a consumer say they were promised repair orders in the mail, it is extremely uncommon to ever hear a consumer say they actually received the work orders in the mail. This is just a ploy to get you to leave without the paperwork, hoping you will forget about it.

Finally, keep the repair orders in a safe place, but not in the glove box of the car! Countless consumers tell of leaving the repair orders in their glove boxes, only to discover that they turned up missing after they had brought the car in for its fourth or fifth repair visit. Service technicians and write up people know that many people keep these documents in the glove box, and if they want to keep the consumer from filing a lemon law complaint or a complaint with someone else, it is a simple matter to remove the papers and throw them away. Even so, if this happened to you, the documents can be recovered, but the process may require litigation and will slow your case's progress down.

I am not sure what drives dealership personnel to do many of the things they do. I have had many clients tell me that not only did the mechanics or managers at the dealership go through their glove boxes and remove all their paperwork, they have even admitted it! More than one client has been accused of not having regular oil changes performed because a service manager took out all the client's papers and—assuming that every paper for the car would be in the glove box—determined that some oil changes were "missed" because the receipts couldn't be found. The dealer hadn't asked the client for permission to dig through the glove box and hadn't even asked if the client had the receipts at home. Obviously, you are better off taking all the documents out of your glove box and keeping them at home.

Used Car Tips

Although the main focus of this book is to address lemon laws and automobile warranties, it would be remiss not to mention a few of the more useful hints about buying a used car. People often wonder what they can do to determine the quality of a used car, especially one that is being purchased from a car lot where the previous owner is unknown. There are several easy things you can do, including track down and speak with the previous owner.

First, if the vehicle is a late model car you should be aware that most automakers have their warranty histories computerized by vehicle identification number. That is, someone—usually a car dealer—with access to the company's warranty system can punch in a VIN and tell you what the repair history of the car has been, at least the paid warranty repairs to date. If, for instance, you were buying a used Dodge automobile from a Chrysler dealer, you should be able to ask the salesperson to print the repair history out for you then and there. If they refuse to do that, or tell you that it can't be done, go shop elsewhere. Their refusal to turn over the history means that they are unscrupulous, know something bad about the car's past, or both. Further, the computer system will tell you if there are any outstanding recalls on the car—that is, if the car has been recalled by the manufacturer but the work has not been performed yet. This would be an indication that the car needs work and that the previous owner ignored recall notices, probably an indication that the owner did not take proper care of the auto.

You may then want to consider tracking the ownership history of the car. Depending on what state you live in, this can be done swiftly and cheaply. Some states will provide you this history for a few dollars and in only a few days. If the car you are looking at is on a used car lot, it will probably be there long enough for you to track the history in time to use your information to aid you in making the purchase.

Merely knowing the prior owner's identity can be quite helpful. For instance, you may discover that the previous owner was a car rental agency. If this is the case, you can guess that the car was bought at auction by the dealer for a very low price, since people in the industry know that former rental cars are very unreliable used cars. They often have an abused past, but the dealers buy them and then sell them without disclosing the rental history past since the cars often look nice and are fairly low mileage. You are better off not buying such a car if you can avoid it.

Further, many rental cars are purchased by the rental companies as "fleet" cars. Many people are unaware that rental companies negotiate bulk car purchases from the manufacturers and as part of the bargain, the manufacturer can build the car to lower standards. A "fleet" vehicle often has less sound deadening in the doors, cheaper upholstery and sometimes fleet cars even have substandard paint jobs. Haven't you ever wondered why rental vehicles are so often rattle traps? It's not just that they are abused; they are built that way!

If the prior owner was an individual you may consider speaking with them, letting them know that you are considering buying the car and want to know if there is anything about the car that you should know. Since the dealer is the one selling the car, a prior owner shouldn't have any problem speaking with you about the car, although some people don't like speaking to strangers about anything. Still, it's worth a shot.

If the prior owner is an insurance company, you quite likely have a seriously damaged car in front of you. Insurance companies acquire titles to cars that they deem total losses and sell them at auction for scrap. Many of these cars have suffered severe collision damage, fire or flood damage, or have been stolen and stripped. Some unscrupulous car dealers buy them at auction, repair them to look nice, and then sell them without disclosing the damaged history. These cars should be avoided at all costs as they are not worth the money and they may even pose a safety hazard to someone driving such a car.

Buying a Car on the Internet

One of the biggest changes to occur in this field in recent years is the advent of the internet when it comes to auto sales. A surprisingly large number of people do their car shopping on line. Car dealers list their inventory on the net and people think nothing of buying or selling used cars on auction sites like Ebay.

The internet is a minefield for unwary consumers who are car shopping. Every attorney in this arena has heard more than enough stories to recognize how precarious on-line car shopping can be. It seems that people have become so comfortable with the internet that they throw common sense out the window.

If you saw a classified ad for a car in the newspaper, would you be comfortable buying the car sight-unseen from the seller without taking it for a test drive? Of course not. Yet, many people will buy a car based upon the modern day equivalent: the internet listing with photographs. First of all, who's to say the photos you see on the internet are of the actual car for sale? I have had consumers call me after a car was delivered to them which was clearly not the car in the internet ad. Or, cars that were damaged and the photos didn't show the damage. Often, the problems would have been revealed by a simple inspection. The problem? The seller was a couple of states away and the buyer trusted the ad and the seller.

My advice? Never buy a car off the internet without doing all of the things you would do in any other auto purchase. Go see the car before you commit to buying it. If you want to skip this step, just assume the worst and price the car accordingly. The car might be wrecked, might not be the one in the picture, it might be stolen. Who knows?

What about the insurance programs where the auction sites claim to stand behind the car sales made on their sites? I've got news for you on that too. Those are simply insurance policies that the auction sites buy and if you file a claim—I know because I've filed one for a client—you will find yourself in a battle with an insurance company, not the auction site. The auction site will wash its hands of you and tell you that your problem is with the insurance company. The insurance company will squirm itself out of any liability to the point where you will wish you had taken my advice to heart: Inspect the car in person before you commit to the purchase!

If you're going to insist on throwing caution to the wind and buy a car on the internet, there are some things you can do to lessen the damage. The first thing is to make sure you save a copy of the listing. Hit "Print" and print a copy of the screen view of the advertisement or listing as it appeared at the time you made the purchase. I have spoken to people who bought a car off the internet and mailed a cashier's check across the country without bothering to print off a copy of the ad that got them to send their money. Later, when the argument happened, the advertisement or listing was gone. How do you prove what the seller promised you when you no longer have a copy of what they said?

Will it help if you are buying a car from a dealer instead of an individual? No. I've seen a dealer who posted four dozen photographs of a very expensive vehicle, but it turned out they were taken of another, undamaged vehicle. As you might guess, a damaged vehicle was shipped to my client. Later, when we proved what had happened—my client saved the screen shots—the dealer claimed it was an understandable error. After all, they had a dozen cars on the lot just like this one and they "accidentally" used the photos of the undamaged car in the ad for the damaged car (which they also "accidentally forgot" to describe as damaged).

If anything, the internet is a much more dangerous place than anywhere else to buy a car. Many unscrupulous sellers believe the distance between themselves and the buyers will protect them. They *want* buyers from out of state and from as far away as possible, hoping the distance will keep the angry buyers from being able to do something about the scam.

The Things Salespeople Say

Salespeople will say almost anything to sell an automobile. After a while, the lines start to sound tired from an attorney's viewpoint, but the lies remain the same: since most car shoppers only buy a car every few years, they don't hear the lines that often. Here is a collection of some of the more common things said by car salespeople. When you hear them: know that they are lying. If you like, show them this book. Maybe even walk away. But, whatever you do—DO NOT believe them!

"This is the last one [car like this] available in the area." Car shoppers hear this line each time they are looking at a car when there is not another car like it on that lot. Salespeople will boldly tell you that a car "this color," or even "with these options," is rare and that this is the "last one," in the area or even the state. Tell him or her that you will double check that and come back if he's telling the truth. Watch him panic and try to stop you as you leave. This is America! You can bet that there are many more just like it at other lots, and probably a hundred more like it rolling off the assembly line each day. Then, test his statement: go to another dealer, and ask them to do a search for you on that type of car with your specifications in mind. They will turn up the first car you just looked at, as well as all the others in the area.

"Your trade-in is worth exactly what you owe on it (or less)." NEVER tell the salesperson what you owe on your car when you are going to trade it in. If necessary, imply that you do not know what you owe on it, and DO NOT tell them where the loan is held (as they will often look it up without telling you). Once they know that you owe, say $5,000 on your trade-in, they will come in with the "good news" that your trade in is worth $5,000—knowing that many people are just happy to get out of their old car without owing any money. To avoid this problem, find out what your loan payoff is before you go shopping. Then, find out the trade-in value of your car. Many people refer to this as the "blue-book" value because of the color of the books which dealers use to appraise average resale and trade-in values of automobiles. There are actually many sources for this information and the blue book is only one of them. Much of this information can be found on the Internet and many banks can give you this information as well (or find the book at a library or bookstore.)

"The bank is making us charge you more for the car than we originally promised to sell it to you for." This is a fairly common tactic for a dealer who is selling a car to a person with less than stellar credit. Quite often, such a buyer will agree to pay more if he or she thinks that otherwise the deal might never happen. However, the bank has no say in how much the car costs you. Beware of any price "inflation" after you have struck a deal. Insist that they stick to the price they promised or get up and leave. If you threaten to walk out, the bank will magically agree to the original price.

"The car was owned by someone who took care of it," or, "The car was an executive car." Any time the salesperson makes a statement about the previous owner, be suspicious. You can test this statement by asking them to put it in writing on the purchase order. If the statement is true, they should have no trouble doing just that. If the statement isn't true, you will see the salesperson squirm and tell you that he cannot put those kinds of statements on the purchase order.

All of the lies above work because car buyers often forget that they are in charge of the sales transaction. The car dealer needs you more than you need them, even though the car dealer will always try to make you think that it is the other way around. Never forget that competition in the auto sales industry is stiff, and if you don't like the way one dealer treats you, there are hundreds of other dealers in the area who want your business. You must never forget that you, the buyer, are the hot commodity in the sales transaction—after all, cars are a dime a dozen, figuratively speaking, and more are rolling off the assembly line every minute.

Does the Lemon Law Protect You When You Buy Something Other Than a Car or Truck?

Many lemon laws protect only buyers of new car or trucks. Although some states' lemon laws cover other things such as motorhomes or boats, there are often large ticket items that are not covered in any given state. People often ask, "What if I buy a defective motorhome, boat or some other thing that is not covered by my state's lemon law?" Since your state's lemon law may not apply to such a sale, "Am I out of luck?" The answer is NO, there are many things you still can do if you have purchased a defective product which is not covered by your state's lemon law.

There are two sources of protection which are of great interest to consumers: the Magnuson-Moss Warranty Act and the Unfair and Deceptive Trade Practices Act. Keep these in mind when any product you buy does not perform as it should. The Magnuson Moss Warranty Act ("The Act") is a Federal law that protects buyers of virtually any consumer goods sold in the US which came with an express written warranty. Excerpts of some important sections of the Act are included in the Appendix. This law is sometimes called the "Federal Lemon Law" but do not think that it applies only to cars and trucks. It applies to any consumer goods which cost more than $25.00, if those goods came with a warranty.

Under the Act, a manufacturer may designate its warranties as "Full" or "Limited," but they must do so clearly. If a manufacturer, or someone else who is obligated under the warranty, fails to remedy a defect as spelled out in the warranty after a reasonable number of repair attempts, the Act requires the manufacturer to either refund the purchase price or replace the product.

If the manufacturer refuses to refund or replace as required by the Act, as they often do, you may have to file suit to get satisfaction. However, the law is very strong, and allows you to not only recover your damages, such as your purchase price, but also your attorney fees and court costs. This means that an attorney skilled in this area should be able to evaluate your situation and take your case without charging you any out of pocket fees.

Magnuson-Moss Warranty Act actions have been successfully filed on behalf of people who have bought defective cars, trucks, motorhomes, snowmobiles, personal watercraft, sewing machines, and countless other items. It is truly a powerful act.

The Unfair and Deceptive Trade Practices Act (the "UDTPA") also protects you when you buy something that doesn't work, or when you get tricked, misled or swindled in a transaction. The UDTPA goes by different names in different states: for instance, in Michigan, it is called the Consumer Protection Act. This state law prohibits a whole laundry list of activities, some of which we have discussed above. However, most important for purchasers of defective warranted goods is the provision that makes it illegal to fail to provide "promised benefits." Some state courts have ruled that a warranty is a promised benefit, and that a manufacturer or seller that fails to honor its warranty is violating this section of the UDTPA.

Further, a warranty is not a promise to work on your product; it's a promise that they will fix it. This distinction is important, because otherwise the seller could keep working on your boat or RV, never fix it right, and just waste your time in giving you the runaround.

The UDTPA also usually allows for you to recover your damages (or $250, whichever is greater in many states) as well as your attorney's fees and costs. In some states there is a punitive aspect to the UDTPA, allowing a court to assess extra damages against a merchant who has willfully or intentionally violated the act.

The attorney fee provision means that an attorney skilled in this area should be able to evaluate your situation and take your case without charging you any out of pocket fees.

These two laws have successfully been used by buyers of cars, trucks, boats, RV's, motorcycles, personal watercraft, computers, appliances, furniture, and photocopiers which did not work right. Remember: it doesn't have to be a car or truck. If you own any consumer product which is defective, these other laws will protect you.

Get it in Writing!

One of the most common mistakes that consumers make is that they fail to get important things in writing. Although the admonition to "Get it in writing" seems simple, it appears that the average consumer still feels uncomfortable demanding written promises. However, the law favors written documents and the terms they contain over spoken promises which are hard to prove or enforce.

The best example is a car purchase. We all know that salespeople make many statements to induce you into purchasing a car. Some are vague sales puffery, such as "This is a great car," or "This car runs perfectly." These kinds of statements, even if the salesperson makes them, are probably not actionable; they are subjective statements which the average consumer should know are opinions, and cannot be verified or quantified in any reasonable manner. However, statements such as "This is a one-owner car," or "This car has a brand new transmission," are objective, quantifiable statements, which, if true, a consumer could reasonably be expected to rely upon.

But salespeople seem to make these latter kinds of statements as easily as the first kind. How can a consumer enforce such statements, or prove they were ever made? Although witnesses who overheard the statements might be able to help you out, it would be much easier if the statements were reduced to writing. Keep this in mind: Any time a salesperson says anything to you that you think is important, ask him or her to put it in writing. This is easy at the time of a car purchase. The car dealer always prepares a "Purchase Agreement" which contains all of the terms of the sale. There is no reason that you cannot dictate some of the terms—especially if all you are asking is for them to reduce their own promises to you in writing.

When the salesman says: "This car's engine was just tuned up," ask him: "Could you please write that on the Purchase Agreement?" If he or she won't do it, you know they are not telling you the truth. **There is no good reason for a salesperson to refuse to write a truthful statement on a purchase agreement.** If they tell you they can't because they are not allowed to, ask to speak with the sales manager. If the manager agrees with them, and says that the statements cannot be reduced to writing, get up and walk out. Any reputable dealer will place the objective statements of its salespeople on its Purchase Agreements.

A salesperson trying to close a deal will often tell you that you can reject goods or services after receipt if you decide you don't like them. However, the preprinted purchase order will often not contain such language. Insist that the salesperson write the language into the contract and initial it before you sign or purchase anything. If they won't you know that the salesperson's promise is worthless and unenforceable.

A recent example involved a prospective purchaser of a boat who inspected the boat on a showroom floor and inquired about purchasing. The overzealous salesman asked if he could write up a purchase agreement. The client insisted that she wanted to test drive the boat, and got the salesman to write "Purchase subject to approval after test drive," on the Purchase Agreement. After she test drove the boat, she decided not to buy the boat, but the salesman, seeking his commission, processed the loan papers and submitted them to the bank anyway. The client received a loan booklet in the mail from the bank, which was unaware of the true facts. The dealer denied the existence of the right to back out of the deal. A letter to the bank, along with a copy of the Purchase Agreement showing the right to back out of the deal after the test drive, straightened the problem out. However, without that language on the Purchase Agreement, the client would have been stuck with a boat and a "he said/she said" situation.

Remember: Get it in Writing. Otherwise, the promise might be unenforceable.

Repossessions, Voluntary or Otherwise, Deficiencies and Leases

The issue of repossessions occurs occasionally in the field of lemon law, since many consumers get so frustrated by their defective cars that they stop making their payments. Ceasing payments on a defective vehicle may be an option in some states but it is never a step a consumer should take before consulting with an attorney. Still, some people find themselves in a situation where their automobile might be repossessed either because they cannot afford their payments, or because they have chosen to not make payments for whatever reason.

A consumer who believes or knows that his or her vehicle is about to be repossessed should take every step possible to avoid it. Unfortunately, many consumers don't understand this concept until it is too late. An in-depth knowledge of this arena can save you thousands of dollars and years of frustration.

Lenders have several remedies available to them when the consumer defaults on the loan; a repossession of the automobile quite often is the lender's first step. Although this is a harsh step for the consumer it is the safest remedy for the lender since they secure the collateral—the car—to protect their financial investment. As advised previously, you should read both sides of your loan contract and know what constitutes a default on your loan as well as what remedies the bank has when you default. This could mean that if you are a day late making a payment, your vehicle could be repossessed and the lender is usually not required to notify you of their intent to repossess your vehicle.

Generally speaking, most banks and lenders will not repossess your vehicle if you are merely a day late making a single payment. Usually a pattern of late payments or a complete failure to make a payment will result in a repossession. Most consumers discover the repossession only when they go to get in their car and cannot find it. Many report the vehicles stolen because they do not immediately realize that the vehicle was repossessed. Lenders quite often repossess the cars with stealth since they know that a consumer whose car is about to be repossessed may hide it.

If you read your loan contract thoroughly, you will also find provisions as to what remedies you, the borrower, have when and if your automobile is repossessed. Usually, you will have the right to redeem the vehicle which is discussed in detail below. If you do nothing after your vehicle is repossessed, the bank will probably auction it for a price far below its wholesale value. One of the reasons for this is that the banks' auctions are attended by professional car buyers who know that repossessed vehicles may be damaged and they often are not allowed to even test drive the vehicles before bidding on them. This situation, legal in most states, almost guarantees that your car will be sold for far less than you could have sold it for.

To stop the auction you must redeem the vehicle, if that is one of your options. To do so, you will have to make up your late payments, getting yourself current on the loan, and probably pay the costs which were incurred in repossessing the vehicle. This will include the costs of towing, storage, and the fees of the people who came and took your car. Even though this will cost you a few hundred dollars, maybe even a thousand dollars above and beyond your payment, it is still probably worth it to do so. The few hundred dollars lost here will be small compared to the thousands you will owe the bank after the auction.

The bank has the right to come after you for the deficiency on the loan that exists after they auction your car and apply the proceeds to your loan. Many people assume that if the bank repossesses their vehicle that this will extinguish the borrowers liability to the bank. Many are also surprised that the bank will sell a car for much less than it is worth at auction. As unfair as all of this seems, it is perfectly legal and is also spelled out in great detail in the fine print on your loan contract.

A common scenario goes like this: the consumer buys a $20,000 car and is making $400 a month payments. With only 10 payments left the engine explodes, and he cannot afford to have the engine repaired. He parks the car and considers his options. After buying another car for transportation, he realizes he cannot make payments on both cars. He figures that he can first let the car get repossessed and let the bank worry about selling it and applying the proceeds to payoff the loan since the car is worth $4,000 and that is exactly what he owes on the loan.

The bank repossesses the car, incurring $1,000 in costs and preparation for the auction, where the car is sold for $1,000, even though it has a wholesale value of $4,000. The bank then sends the consumer a bill for $4,000, with a note saying that if he does not pay the $4,000 promptly, they will sue him for it. Further, if he does not pay the amount in question he will likely lose the lawsuit, assuming that the bank followed proper procedures for disposing of the car at auction.

The main requirements the lender must follow are notice requirements. In other words, they have to send letters telling the consumer of his right to redeem, his right to attend the auction—if the law requires the lender to give him this right and an accounting of how they calculated the deficiency. Some states may require other or more notices, but this scenario is all too common and happens every day in this country.

A better scenario for the same consumer would go like this: He borrows a thousand dollars from a friend or relative, gets the engine repaired and then sells the car through the newspaper for $4,000. He has the buyer accompany him to his bank so he can payoff the loan with the $4,000 he gets from the sale and he can give the buyer a clear title. When all is said and done he is only in debt the amount it cost to repair the engine.

A consumer can always realize more money from a private sale of the vehicle than the bank will realize at auction. Again: Never let your vehicle get repossessed if you can avoid it. If it gets repossessed, exercise your right to redeem the vehicle. Sell the vehicle yourself before the bank sells it for you.

Finally, consumers need to realize that repossessions appear on credit reports and some suggest that the only worse things you can have on your credit history are judgments and bankruptcies. Even a voluntary repossession will be a red flag to any lender in the future and will lead them to believe that you are financially irresponsible. This, if for no other reason, this should make you think twice before allowing your automobile to be repossessed.

Lease Termination Repossessions

Many consumers misunderstand their lease contracts and as a result do serious damage to their financial situation if they fall behind in their payments. Most consumers view their leased automobiles as if they were renting the car or truck, when the transaction is better viewed as a purchase. Keep this in mind, even if you do not intend to buy out the lease at the end of its terms. Most leases have default provisions in them that are identical to the default provisions of a loan contract.

In other words, if you stop making your lease payments, the lender usually has the right to repossess the vehicle, sell it at auction, create a deficiency and sue you for the balance. Many people assume that they will only be sued for the unpaid payments on the lease; this is not the case. Examining the situation above, but changing the underlying contract to a lease, the story would read like this: the consumer leases a car with a $20,000 sticker price and a $7,000 residual value and is making $400 a month lease payments. With only 10 payments left the engine explodes, and he cannot afford to have the engine repaired. He parks the car and considers his options. After buying another car for transportation, he realizes he cannot make payments on both cars. He figures that he can let the car get repossessed and let the bank worry about selling it and applying the proceeds to payoff the lease, since the payments he owes only equal $4,000.

The bank repossesses the car, incurring $1,000 in costs and preparation for the auction, where the car is sold for $1,000, even though it has a wholesale value of $4,000. The bank then sends the consumer a bill for $11,000, with a note saying that if he does not pay the $11,000 promptly, they will sue him for it. They will explain their math to him: he owes $4,000 for the missed payments and he owes another $7,000 for the residual value of the automobile which was not covered by the sale price at auction. Further, if he does not pay the amount in question he will likely lose the lawsuit, assuming that the bank followed the proper procedures for disposing of the car at auction. This aspect of leasing is usually the most confusing for the consumer. In most rental situations the lessee is only responsible for making all of their payments, as is the case with real estate transactions. This aspect of leasing, where the bank sells the collateral and makes the consumer pay the shortfall, is very advantageous for the bank and very disadvantageous for the consumer. However, it is the law in most states and it is also exactly what is spelled out in the contract the consumer signed at the time they took delivery of the car.

When Can You Legally Return a Vehicle?

If your vehicle is severely defective and you intend to pursue the lemon law, or if it does not qualify under the lemon law but its warranties are not being honored, you may be able to legally revoke your acceptance of it and return it to the selling dealer. This concept also applies to other consumer goods besides automobiles.

There is much confusion around the issue of when a consumer can return a product to the seller and rightfully demand a refund. In fact, one of the most commonly asked questions that consumer protection attorneys hear is: "When can the consumer return a product and get his or her money back?" And, more importantly, "If they won't refund your money, what do you do then?"

Generally speaking, consumers are protected in most purchases of goods when the products are sold by merchants and the goods aren't sold "as-is." Simply put, a merchant is usually a business, such as a store or a dealer, but can be any person that holds itself out or advertises as dealing in goods of that kind. A Wal-Mart or ACO Hardware is clearly a merchant, as is a car dealer. A person who advertises items or goods for sale often is a merchant.

A person advertising to sell their car in the local paper is not a merchant if they are merely disposing of their personal car. "As-is" sales were discussed previously. This is a very important concept, since so many people buy used cars from individuals. In most states there are no warranties regarding the fitness of the vehicle in this type of sale unless the seller explicitly makes promises that go beyond mere sales puffery. If the seller merely tells you that the car runs fine or that he or she has had few problems with it, you cannot later sue them if the car breaks down. On the other hand, if the seller promised to replace the transmission if it failed within a certain time frame, you could reasonably expect the seller to honor the promise. The problem is that if such a promise is made verbally, it will likely be broken later and be difficult to prove that the promise was made in the first place.

I should point out here that a common scam for a car dealer to run is to advertise a car for sale and make it look like it is being sold by an individual. Many car dealers realize that most buyers trust individuals more than they trust used car salesmen. So, they take out an ad for a car on their lot and list a salesman's cell phone for the contact. If you call on the car, you will be directed to see the car at the salesman's home, or some other nearby residence. If you wind up wanting to buy the car, they will then tell you that the dealer will do the paperwork for you because the dealer is a "friend" doing this as a favor to make the paperwork easier. This is illegal in most states. Most states require dealers to conduct their business at their commercial location. The sales contracts in the transaction I described here would list the dealer as the "seller," which would not make sense if the seller was telling the truth. These transactions occur all the time and very few consumers have the courage to walk away from the transaction once they suspect something is wrong. My advice? Run!

The advantage of buying from a "merchant" is that all sales of goods in most states by merchants are accompanied by an "implied warranty of merchantability." This is the concept that the goods you are buying will be fit for their ordinary purposes. Since it is an "implied" warranty, the merchant does not have to make any statements or promises for this to exist. The implied warranty of merchantability exists on its own. That means that if you buy a refrigerator, it will keep your food cold; a lawnmower will cut grass; a hair dryer will dry your hair. This implied warranty exists along with any other warranties which might come with your product.

Although Implied Warranties don't appear in the paperwork covering warranties, they protect almost every new or used car bought from a dealer. State laws mandate that implied warranties be honored unless the dealer tells you in writing at the time of the sale that they do not apply. There are generally two kinds of implied warranties that you should be aware of. The implied warranty of merchantability guarantees that a product will do what a consumer reasonably expects it to. With respect to a car that means that the vehicle will provide safe and reliable transportation. Constant breakdowns or failure to start regularly may constitute a breach of the implied warranty of merchantability. The "As-is" disclaimer on the Buyer's Guide in an automobile purchase is the only way a merchant can negate the implied warranty of merchantability. This concept is discussed in depth in the section on the Buyer's Guide earlier in this book.

The other kind of warranty that falls into this arena is the warranty of fitness for a particular purpose. This applies if the seller tells you that the product—the vehicle—can perform in a particular manner. So, although the literature may not expressly warrant a truck's ability to pull a trailer of a given weight, if the salesman tells you it can, this statement may create such a warranty. Disputes often arise, however, when a buyer claims that the salesperson promised that the vehicle could pull a trailer of a certain size and the salesman later denies ever having made such a statement. In anticipation of such a defense, be sure to make the salesperson write on the purchase agreement what he tells you the vehicle can accomplish. If he tells you it will pull a 10,000 pound trailer at highway speeds, make him write it down. If he won't write it down, shop elsewhere. A reputable dealer will have no problem putting a truthful statement in writing.

The most important aspect of this is that if your product doesn't work as you reasonably expected, you may revoke acceptance of it and return it to the seller if the seller cannot make the item perform as expected. The same is true if your product came with an express warranty that isn't honored. Many products state that if they fail or are defective, the manufacturer will repair or replace them within certain guidelines. If they do not fulfill that "repair or replace" obligation and you have complied with all of the requirements of the warranty, you can demand a refund as well. This concept does not apply to the "as-is" sale from a private individual.

Although the term "revocation of acceptance" sounds legalistic, it stands for the simple concept that you can return a defective product for a refund. To rightfully revoke acceptance of the defective product you must act within a reasonable amount of time and before any substantial wear and tear of the item occurs which is not the result of the defect. A "reasonable" time is not defined within the law, but it would be safe to say that as soon as you discover the defect, you should plan on returning the item at your next opportunity. For an item to not substantially change in condition means that you cannot use the item or wear it out before returning it. It would probably be a good idea to not use the item at all once you have discovered the need to return it. Otherwise, the merchant might argue that your use of it proves that the item wasn't defective or that your continued use of the defective item caused more harm.

Be aware that these aspects of the law cover all purchases of goods, and goods can be anything from the home appliances to automobiles. Car dealers do not want you to know this! Most consumers who have tried to return defective cars to selling dealers describe harrowing experiences and arguments with salespeople and managers who threaten to call the police or have the cars towed away as "abandoned." Beware: car dealers are experienced in this field, and take extra precautions when selling their merchandise. Often, they do this "as-is;" some statistics suggest that more than ninety percent of all used cars sold in the U.S. are sold "as-is."

However, there may be situations where even a car sold "as-is" can rightfully be returned to a seller for a full refund. Keeping in mind that the "as-is" disclaimer only disclaims the implied warranties, fraud in the sale or violation of a statute may give rise to your right to revoke. For example, suppose a car dealer rolled an odometer back before selling a car to you. Even if the car was sold "as-is" the seller violated a Federal statute on odometer tampering, which the "as-is" disclaimer does not impact. In that instance, the "as-is" disclaimer would do nothing to protect the seller from your claims against him.

If you rightfully revoke your acceptance of the product, of whatever kind, the merchant must refund your money to you. If they don't they are probably violating your state's UDTPA. Most of those acts specifically prohibit failing to refund the consumer's money in a transaction that is rightfully canceled or rescinded. If you had returned the item to the seller properly, and they refused to refund your money (or trade-in if you traded a car in on another, for example), you could sue them under this Act and if you won, you would be entitled to a full refund. Further, if you won, the merchant may have to pay your attorney fees and court costs for the action.

You should always consult an attorney before taking the drastic step of revoking acceptance of a product if the merchant does not agree to refund your money when you do so. In those instances a lawsuit is often necessary to recover your money anyway, and there may be additional actions you should take at that time to protect your interests adequately.

Don't I Have Three Days to Return the Vehicle If I Don't Like It?

Many consumers mistakenly believe that they have three days to cancel any contract they sign, or three days to return anything they buy "No questions asked." There are very few situations where this concept applies and it almost never applies to cars! Even if a salesman tells you that you can return the car in three days no questions asked, do not believe him or her unless they put that promise in writing.

The three day "cooling off" period arises from a Federal Trade Commission guideline which generally applies to sales that take place in your home. Think of a traveling salesman who comes to your house, knocks on the door and tries to sell you a vacuum cleaner. If your first contact with the salesman or his company was when he knocked on your door, you will have three days from when he leaves to cancel any contract you signed while he was present. The law also requires the salesman to provide you with a written form which advises you of this right. However, the law does not apply to a sale that takes place at a used or new car lot.

Consumer attorneys are asked this question so often that it is apparently one of the most misunderstood areas in the law. Consumers will call an attorney's office, frantic because they bought a car two and a half days earlier, and want to know how to invoke this mysterious law before the three days are up. Sadly, no such right exists.

Complaining More Effectively

Many consumers are inspired to write letters of complaint regarding their defective automobiles to everyone from the president of the manufacturer, to the attorney general of their state, to the news anchor of the local newscast. Although these letters may relieve some of the pent up hostilities you feel toward the people responsible for the defective auto, most attorneys will advise against sending such letters. There are several reasons for this.

Obviously, this does not change what was stated earlier about last chance letters. Those should be sent as described previously, but note how business-like and straight forward the model letter is. The letters being addressed in this chapter are the kind where consumers want to vent their anger.

Why not send an angry letter to the president of the automobile manufacturer? First, it risks making you look unbalanced. A letter that was fun to write in the privacy of your own home looks different when introduced during litigation. Consumers usually regret having sent the letter when it is pulled out and displayed to judges, jurors, or even other attorneys. If the letter was written with much vehemence, it will likely suggest that you are irrational, angry, or any number of other things you do not want to be accused of. You are merely a consumer who wants to get what you paid for.

Next, the letter will not get you anywhere. Presidents of large corporations have secretaries whose job it is to sort incoming mail into what politely can be called the important mail and the unimportant mail. The unimportant mail, including the hate mail and correspondence of the disgruntled is sent to someone in customer service who then responds with a form letter stating that although they are disappointed that you are having a bad experience with their product, they can only suggest that you continue working with your dealership. Never in the history of mankind has the president of a large corporation even seen such a letter, let alone responded to one.

Attorneys general are overworked, underpaid government servants who spend their time trying as best they can to protect the consumers of their state from the widespread abuses that run rampant through modern America. Most receive complaints and file them, after sending a copy of the complaint to the merchant, with a request that the merchant respond to the claim of the consumer. In many states, if the merchant merely responds, the case is closed. There are enough unscrupulous merchants out there who do not respond to requests of the attorney general to keep his or her staff busy for decades. And, as you may guess, large manufacturers have personnel whose only job is to respond to the requests from the attorneys general to make sure that no follow up is required or done by the state.

Although there is nothing wrong with filing a complaint with the state where you live, it will generally accomplish nothing on your behalf. It will waste a few minutes of the attorney general's staff's time and will document that you have a complaint. However, as with the hate mail to the president of the company, beware that a copy of your complaint will be sent to the manufacturer. If there is anything in your letter which may hurt your case, they will use it against you. Because of that, I advise clients to avoid sending complaint letters to the state unless they really have a burning desire to do so. If so, do it politely and don't get your hopes up.

It has become a common belief in our society that complaints to news organizations scare merchants into compliance with the law. Consumer attorneys all too often hear the refrain, "I'll call the news," as if that is a bigger threat than litigation. From someone who has worked in the media for twenty years, you can be sure that this is the furthest thing from the truth. News organizations are bombarded with requests of a similar nature, on a daily basis in some instances. By definition, this is not news. Television, radio and newspapers are looking for newsworthy stories that either interest or affect many of their viewers, listeners, or readers. That you are unhappy with your car is not news. At most, you will make your statement and the professional spokesperson from the automaker will make a counter-statement in which they will look better than you since that's what they do for a living.

Finally, be aware that some auto makers value their reputation to the point that they may attack you if you are not careful what you say or who you say it to. If you make a false or disparaging statement about an automaker, they may be inclined to sue you for slander. Without going into the definitions of slander or the various ramifications to you if you do it, rest assured that the automaker has literally hundreds, if not thousands, of attorneys at its disposal. It takes no more than a phone call to one of them to have you hauled into court to defend a slander action.

Whether or not you would win such a suit, you probably can't afford it. You are better off with an attorney handling your lemon law claim, and doing your speaking for you in the courtroom if it goes that far.

Appendix A
Sample Last Chance Letter

Here is an example of a last chance letter. If your state's lemon law requires one, you can use this as a guide. Retype the letter below and fill in the blanks.

SEND THIS CERTIFIED—RETURN RECEIPT REQUESTED!
<u>SAVE A COPY FOR YOUR RECORDS</u>

Your Home Address
Your Home Telephone Number
Your Work Telephone Number

Name of Manufacturer
Manufacturer's Address

Dear Sir or Madam:

I believe my car/truck is a "lemon" under my state's lemon law. I hereby demand relief under the Lemon Law and the Uniform Commercial Code.

I purchased a (make, model, year of vehicle) on (date) from (name of dealership) in (city, state). The vehicle identification number or VIN number is (vehicle identification number). Since purchase, I have had to return it to the dealership a total of (number of times the vehicle was returned to an authorized dealer for repairs) times. My vehicle has been out of service for repairs for a total of (total number of business days the vehicle has been out of service being repaired) business days. I am currently having the following problems with my vehicle at this time: (list all problems the vehicle currently has).

These defects substantially impair the use/value of my vehicle. I am hereby allowing you one final repair opportunity. If these repairs are not completed within seven
business days of receipt of this letter I am entitled to a replacement vehicle acceptable to me or a refund calculated in accordance with the Lemon Law.

I look forward to hearing from you soon.

Sincerely,
Your Name

Appendix B
Internet Resources

There is a wealth of information on the Internet for consumers with questions regarding their automobile and warranty law. The following is not intended to be exhaustive, it is merely a list of the sites that prove most informative and useful.

is the government sponsored site of the National Highway Transportation Safety Administration. NHTSA tracks all automobile recalls as well as technical service bulletins issued by any manufacturer that sells vehicle in the United States. These two items are vitally important to all consumers.

Recalls are mandated by NHTSA whenever a safety related defect has been discovered in a particular model of automobile. Usually, when a recall is issued, the manufacturer will send a notice to the owners of the autos in question telling them of the defect and where and when they can get it repaired free of charge. However, if you are not the original owner of the car, it is possible that the notice went to the prior owner and you could be driving a car with a serious manufacturing defect and not know it. Literally within seconds, the NHTSA will tell you of any recalls for your make and model of car or truck. The site is very easy to use, allowing you to select from pull-down menus so that you are sure that you are looking at the correct information.

Likewise, the NHTSA site tracks technical service bulletins. TSBs are the official reports that manufacturers issue to their dealers informing them of known problems with particular cars or trucks and how they can be fixed. The review of TSBs can be extremely helpful to a consumer for several reasons. First, it is not uncommon for a dealer to give your concern short shrift if it is difficult to diagnose. Although they make money doing warranty repairs, dealers sometimes do not get paid if they are doing repetitive work on the same car over and over again. If you get this treatment from a dealer, you can look to see if there are TSBs that they might not be aware of. Many consumers tell of finding TSBs for their autos, and then being told by the dealer that this was the first that they had heard of the problem. This is indicative of lazy dealer personnel, since TSBs are available at the push of a button to service technicians at dealerships.

Second, the TSBs can be used to bolster your lemon law claim. Not all TSB fixes work. Quite often the TSB will suggest ways to try and fix some problem and dealers report that the problem persists. If you have met disbelief from the dealer, perhaps they have NPF'd your car with respect to your complaint, a TSB goes a long way toward showing that such a problem does in fact exist.

Also, as discussed previously, some manufacturers will quibble about how serious a defect is and whether or not it impairs the use or value of the automobile in question. If a TSB exists describing the problem, the consumer can argue that the problem must impair the use or value of the vehicle. Otherwise, why would the manufacturer bother issuing a technical service bulletin to solve it?

The Internet site is useful to consumers looking for an attorney. Here is a list of attorneys cross referenced by state as well as by specialty. If there is an attorney near you who practices lemon law, you should be able to locate them here. Access to the site is free; it is paid for by the attorneys who pay a fee for being listed.

Appendix C
Lemon Laws Around the Nation

The following is a list of the citations for the various automobile warranty laws from around the U.S. Since laws change all the time, we have not attempted to summarize the statutes here. This list will allow you to locate the law if you so desire, or at least allow you to point it out to an attorney, should you consult with one who is unfamiliar with the law.

Also remember that each state has adopted the Uniform Commercial Code in some form, and all attorneys studied it in law school—at least the ones who attended law school after the UCC was adopted. The UCC is the source for warranty law in general, with regard to any products. Your state may also have adopted a version of the Uniform Deceptive Trade Practices Act, calling it a Consumer Protection Act or something similar. Examine all three sources of law when considering action over a defective product, keeping in mind that the latter two are not limited or restricted to automobiles.

—

Alabama §8-20A-1 *et seq.*

§8-20A-1(c) It shall be presumed that reasonable attempts to correct a nonconforming condition have been allowed by the consumer if, during the period of 24 months following delivery of the vehicle or 24,000 miles, whichever first occurs, either of the following events shall have occurred:

(1) The same nonconforming condition has been subject to repair attempts three or more times by the manufacturer, its agents or its authorized dealers, at least one of which occurred during the lemon law rights period, plus a final attempt by the manufacturer, and the same nonconforming condition continues to exist; or

(2) The motor vehicle is out of service and in the custody of the manufacturer, its agent, or an authorized dealer due to repair attempts (including the final repair attempt), one of which occurred during the lemon law rights period, for a cumulative total of 30 calendar days, unless such repair could not be performed because of conditions beyond the control of the manufacturer, its agents or authorized dealers, such as war, invasion, strike, fire, flood, or other natural disaster.

Alaska §45.45.300 *et seq.*

§45.45.320 A presumption that a reasonable number of attempts have been made to conform a motor vehicle under an applicable express warranty is established if:

(1) the same nonconformity has been subject to repair three or more times by the manufacturer, distributor, dealer, or repairing agent during the term of the express warranty or the one-year period after delivery of the motor vehicle to the original owner, whichever period terminates first, but the nonconformity continues to exist; or,

(2) the vehicle is out of service for repair for a total of 30 or more business days during the express warranty term or the one-year period referred to in (1) of this section, whichever period terminates first; any period of time that repairs are not performed for reasons that are beyond the control of the manufacturer, distributor, dealer, or repairing agent is excluded from the 30-day time period referred to in this paragraph.

Arizona §44-1261 *et seq.*

§44-1264(A) It is presumed that a reasonable number of attempts have been undertaken to conform a motor vehicle to the applicable express warranties if either:

1. The same nonconformity has been subject to repair four or more times by the manufacturer or its agents or authorized dealers during the shorter of the express warranty term or the period of two years or twenty-four thousand miles following the date of original delivery of the motor vehicle to the consumer, whichever is earlier, but the nonconformity continues to exist.

2. The motor vehicle is out of service by reason of repair for a cumulative total of thirty or more calendar days during the shorter of the express warranty term or the two year period or twenty-four thousand miles, whichever is earlier.

Arkansas §4-90-401 *et seq.*

§ 4-90-410(a) A rebuttable presumption of a reasonable number of attempts to repair is considered to have been undertaken to correct a nonconformity if:

(1) The nonconformity has been subject to repair as provided in § 4-90-406(a), but the nonconformity continues to exist;

(2) The vehicle is out of service by reason of repair, or attempt to repair, any nonconformity for a cumulative total of thirty (30) calendar days; or

(3) There have been five (5) or more attempts, on separate occasions, to repair any nonconformities that together substantially impair the use and value of the motor vehicle to the consumer.

California §1793.22 *et seq.*

1793.22(b) It shall be presumed that a reasonable number of attempts have been made to conform a new motor vehicle to the applicable express warranties if, within one year from delivery to the buyer or 12,000 miles on the odometer of the vehicle, whichever occurs first, either

(1) the same nonconformity has been subject to repair four or more times by the manufacturer or its agents and the buyer has at least once directly notified the manufacturer of the need for the repair of the nonconformity or,

(2) the vehicle is out of service by reason of repair of nonconformities by the manufacturer or its agents for a cumulative total of more than 30 calendar days since delivery of the vehicle to the buyer. The 30-day limit shall be extended only if repairs cannot be performed due to conditions beyond the control of the manufacturer or its agents. The buyer shall be required to directly notify the manufacturer pursuant to paragraph (1) only if the manufacturer has clearly and conspicuously disclosed to the buyer, with the warranty or the owner's manual, the provisions of this section and that of subdivision (d) of Section 1793.2, including the requirement that the buyer must notify the manufacturer directly pursuant to paragraph (1). This presumption shall be a rebuttable presumption affecting the burden of proof, and it may be asserted by the buyer in any civil action, including an action in small claims court, or other formal or informal proceeding.

Colorado §42-10-101 *et seq.*

42-10-102(a) It shall be presumed that a reasonable number of attempts have been undertaken to conform a motor vehicle to the warranty if:

(I) The same nonconformity has been subject to repair four or more times by the manufacturer, its agent, or its authorized dealer within the warranty term or during a period of one year following the date of the original delivery of the motor vehicle to the consumer, whichever is the earlier date, but such nonconformity continues to exist; or,

(II) The motor vehicle is out of service by reason of repair for a cumulative total of thirty or more business days of the repairer during the term specified in subparagraph (I) of this paragraph (a) or during the period specified in said subparagraph (I), whichever is earlier.

Connecticut §42-179a *et seq.*

§42-179(e) It shall be presumed that a reasonable number of attempts have been undertaken to conform a motor vehicle to the applicable express warranties, if:

(1) the same nonconformity has been subject to repair four or more times by the manufacturer or its agents or authorized dealers during the period of two years following the date of original delivery of the motor vehicle to a consumer or during the period of the first eighteen thousand miles of operation, whichever period ends first, but such nonconformity continues to exist or,

(2) the vehicle is out of service by reason of repair for a cumulative total of thirty or more calendar days during the applicable period, determined pursuant to subdivision (1) of this subsection. Such two-year period and such thirty-day period shall be extended by any period of time during which repair services are not available to the consumer because of a war, invasion, strike or fire, flood or other natural disaster. No claim shall be made under this section unless at least one attempt to repair a nonconformity has been made by the manufacturer or its agent or an au-

thorized dealer or unless such manufacturer, its agent or an authorized dealer has refused to attempt to repair such nonconformity.

Delaware Title 6, sub II, chapter 50, §5001 *et seq.*

§ 5004(a) It shall be presumed that a reasonable number of attempts have been undertaken to conform a new automobile to the manufacturer's express warranty if, within the warranty term or during the period of 1 year following the date of original delivery of the motor vehicle to a consumer, whichever is the earlier date:

(1) Substantially the same nonconformity has been subject to repair or correction 4 or more times by the manufacturer, its agents or its dealers and the nonconformity continues to exist; or,

(2) The automobile is out of service by reason of repair or correction of a nonconformity by the manufacturer, its agents or its dealers for a cumulative total of more than 30 calendar days since the original delivery of the motor vehicle to the consumer. This 30-day limit shall commence with the first day on which the consumer presents the automobile to the manufacturer, its agent or dealer for service of the nonconformity and a written document describing the nonconformity is prepared by the manufacturer, its agent or dealer. The 30-day limit shall be extended only if repairs cannot be performed due to conditions beyond the control of the manufacturer, its agents or its dealers, including war, invasion, strike, fire, flood or other natural disaster.

Florida §681.10 *et seq.*

It is presumed that a reasonable number of attempts have been undertaken to conform a motor vehicle to the warranty if, during the Lemon Law rights period, either:

(a) The same nonconformity has been subject to repair at least three times by the manufacturer or its authorized service agent, plus a final attempt by the manufacturer to repair the motor vehicle if undertaken as provided for in paragraph (1)(a), and such nonconformity continues to exist; or,

(b) The motor vehicle has been out of service by reason of repair of one or more nonconformities by the manufacturer, or its authorized service agent, for a cumulative total of 30 or more days, 60 or more days in the case of a recreational vehicle, exclusive of downtime for routine maintenance prescribed by the owner's manual. The manufacturer or its authorized service agent must have had at least one opportunity to inspect or repair the vehicle following receipt of the notification as provided in paragraph (1)(b). The 30-day period, or 60-day period in the case of a recreational vehicle, may be extended by any period of time during which repair services are not available to the consumer because of war, invasion, strike, fire, flood, or natural disaster.

Georgia §10-1-780 *et seq.*

10-1-784(b) A reasonable number of attempts shall be presumed as a matter of law to have been undertaken by the manufacturer, its agent, or the new motor vehicle dealer to repair or correct any nonconformity of a new motor vehicle, if:

(1) a serious safety defect in the braking or steering system has been subject to repair at least once during the lemon law rights period and has not been corrected; [or]

(2) during any period of 24 months or less, or during any period in which the vehicle has been driven 24,000 miles or less, whichever occurs first, any other serious safety defect has been subject to repair two or more times, at least one of which is during the lemon law rights period, and the nonconformity continues to exist; [or]

(3) during any period of 24 months or less or during any period in which the vehicle has been driven 24,000 miles or less, whichever occurs first, the same nonconformity has been subject to repair, three or more times, at least one of which is during the lemon law rights period, and the nonconformity continues to exist; or

(4) during any period of 24 months or less or during any period in which the vehicle has been driven 24,000 miles or less, whichever occurs first, the vehicle is out of service by reason of repair of one or more nonconformities for a cumulative total of 30 calendar days, at least 15 of them during the lemon law rights period. If less than 15 days remain under the lemon law rights period when the new motor vehicle is first brought in for diagnosis or repair, the lemon law rights period as regards

the problem to be diagnosed or repaired shall be extended for a period of 90 days.

Hawaii §4811-1 *et seq.*

§4811-3(d) It shall be presumed that a reasonable number of attempts have been undertaken to conform a motor vehicle to the applicable express warranties, if, during the lemon law rights period, any of the following occurs:

(1) The same nonconformity has been subject to examination or repair at least three times by the manufacturer, its agents, distributors, or authorized dealers, but such nonconformity continues to exists; or

(2) The nonconformity has been subject to examination or repair at least once by the manufacturer, its agents, distributors, or authorized dealers, but continues to be a nonconformity which is likely to cause death or serious bodily injury if the vehicle is driven; or

(3) The motor vehicle is out of service by reason of repair by the manufacturer, its agents, distributors, or authorized dealers for one or more nonconformities for a cumulative total of thirty or more business days during the lemon law rights period. The term of the lemon law rights period and such thirty-day period shall be extended by any period of time during which repair services are not available to the consumer because of a war, invasion, strike, fire, flood or other natural disaster.

Idaho §48-901 *et seq.*

48-902(2) It is presumed that a reasonable number of attempts have been undertaken to conform a new motor vehicle to the applicable express warranties, if

(a) the same nonconformity has been subject to repair four (4) or more times by the manufacturer, its agents, or its authorized dealers within the applicable express warranty term or during the period of two (2) years following the date of original delivery of the new motor vehicle to a consumer or during the period ending with the date on which the mileage on the motor vehicle reaches twenty-four thousand (24,000) miles, whichever is the earliest date, but the nonconformity continues to exist. However, the manufacturer shall have at least one (1) opportunity to attempt to repair the vehicle before it is presumed a reasonable number of attempts have been undertaken to conform the vehicle to the applicable express warranty; or

(b) the vehicle is out of service by reason of repair for a cumulative total of thirty (30) or more business days during the term or during the period, whichever is the earlier date.

(3) If the nonconformity results in a complete failure of the braking or steering system of the new motor vehicle and is likely to cause death or serious bodily injury if the vehicle is driven, it is presumed that a reasonable number of attempts have been undertaken to conform the vehicle to the applicable express warranties if the nonconformity has been subject to repair at least once by the manufacturer, its agents, or its authorized dealers within the applicable express warranty term or during the period of two (2) years following the date of original delivery of the new motor vehicle to a consumer or during the period ending with the date on which the mileage on the motor vehicle reaches twenty-four thousand (24,000) miles, whichever is the earliest date, and the nonconformity continues to exist. However, the manufacturer shall have at least one (1) opportunity to attempt to repair the vehicle before it is presumed a reasonable number of attempts have been undertaken to conform the vehicle to the applicable express warranty.

Illinois §815.380.1 *et seq.*

815.380.3(b) A presumption that a reasonable number of attempts have been undertaken to conform a new vehicle to its express warranties shall arise where, within the statutory warranty period,

(1) the same nonconformity has been subject to repair by the seller, its agents or authorized dealers during the statutory warranty period, 4 or more times, and such nonconformity continues to exist; or,

(2) the vehicle has been out of service by reason of repair of nonconformities for a total of 30 or more business days during the statutory warranty period.

Indiana §24-5-13-1 *et seq.*

§24-5-13-15(a) A reasonable number of attempts is considered to have been undertaken to correct
a nonconformity if:

(1) the nonconformity has been subject to repair at least four (4) times by the manufacturer or its agents or authorized dealers, but the nonconformity continues to exist; or,

(2) the vehicle is out of service by reason of repair of any nonconformity for a cumulative total of at least thirty (30) business days, and the nonconformity continues to exist.

Iowa §322G.1 *et seq.*

322G.4(3) It is presumed that a reasonable number of attempts have been undertaken to conform a motor vehicle to the warranty if, during the lemon law rights period, any of the following occur:

a. The same nonconformity that substantially impairs the motor vehicle has been subject to examination or repair at least three times by the manufacturer or its authorized service agent, plus a final attempt by the manufacturer to repair the motor vehicle if undertaken as provided for in subsection 1, and such nonconformity continues to exist. [or]

b. A nonconformity that is likely to cause death or serious bodily injury has been subject to examination or repair at least one time by the manufacturer or its authorized service agent, plus a final attempt by the manufacturer to repair the motor vehicle if undertaken as provided for in subsection 1, and such nonconformity continues to exist. [or]

c. The motor vehicle has been out of service by reason of repair by the manufacturer, or its authorized service agent, of one or more nonconformities that substantially impair the motor vehicle for a cumulative total of thirty or more days, exclusive of down time for routine maintenance prescribed by the owner's manual. The thirty-day period may be extended by any period of time during which repair services are not available to the consumer because of war, invasion, strike, fire, flood, or natural disaster.

Kansas §50-645 *et seq.*

§50-645 (d) If the manufacturer receives actual notice of the nonconformity, it shall be presumed

that a reasonable number of attempts have been undertaken to conform a motor vehicle to the applicable warranties, if:

(1) The same nonconformity which substantially impairs the use and value of the motor vehicle to the consumer has been subject to repair four or more times by the manufacturer or its agents or authorized dealers within the term of any warranty or during the period of one year following the date of original delivery of the motor vehicle to a consumer, whichever is the earlier date, but such nonconformity continues to exist; [or]

(2) the vehicle is out of service by reason of repair for a cumulative total of 30 or more calendar days during such term or period, whichever is the earlier date; or,

(3) there have been 10 or more attempts to repair any nonconformities which substantially impair the use and value of the motor vehicle to the consumer and such attempts to repair have been attempts by the manufacturer or its agents or authorized dealers.

Kentucky §367.840 *et seq.*

367.842(3) It shall be presumed that a reasonable number of attempts have been undertaken to conform a motor vehicle to the applicable express warranty if, within the first twelve thousand (12,000) miles of operation or during the period of, twelve (12) months following the date of original delivery of the motor vehicle to the buyer, whichever is the earlier date:

(a) The same nonconformity, defect, or condition has been subject to repair four (4) or more times by the manufacturer, but such nonconformity, defect, or condition continues to exist; or

(b) The vehicle is out of service/use by reason of repair of the same nonconformity, defect, or condition for a cumulative total of at least thirty (30) calendar days.

Louisiana §5-1941 *et seq.*

If after four or more attempts within the express warranty term or during a period of one year following the date of the original delivery of the motor vehicle to you, whichever is earlier, the nonconformity has not been repaired or if the vehicle is out of service by reason of repair for a cumulative total of 30 or more days during the warranty period, the manufacturer shall do one of two things:

(1) Replace the motor vehicle with a comparable new motor vehicle, or, at its option;

(2) Accept return of the motor vehicle and refund the full purchase price plus any amounts paid by the consumer at the point of sale, and all collateral costs less a reasonable allowance for use.

Massachusetts §90:7N.50 *et seq.*

§90:7N.50(4) A reasonable number of attempts shall be deemed to have been undertaken to conform a motor vehicle to any applicable express or implied warranties if:

(a) the same nonconformity has been subject to repair three or more times by the manufacturer or its agents or authorized dealers within the term of protection, but such nonconformity continues to exist or such nonconformity has recurred within the term of protection, or,

(b) the vehicle is out of service by reason of repair of any nonconformity for a cumulative total of fifteen or more business days during the term of protection; provided, however, that the manufacturer shall be afforded one additional opportunity, not to exceed seven business days, to cure any nonconformity arising during the term of protection, notwithstanding the fact that such additional opportunity to cure commences after the term of protection. Such additional opportunity to cure shall commence on the day the manufacturer first knows or should have known that the limits specified in clause (a) or (b) have been met or exceeded.

Maine Chapter 203-A, Title 10 §1161 *et seq.*

§1163. Reasonable number of attempts; presumption. There is a presumption that a reasonable number of attempts have been undertaken to conform a motor vehicle to the applicable express warranties if:

A. The same nonconformity has been subject to repair 3 or more times by the manufacturer or its agents or authorized dealers within the express warranty term, during the period of 2 years following the date of original delivery of the motor vehicle to a consumer or during the first 18,000 miles of operation, whichever is the earlier date, and at least 2 of those times the same agent or dealer attempted the repair but the nonconformity continues to exist; or,

B. The vehicle is out of service by reason of repair by the manufacturer, its agents or authorized dealer, of any defect or condition or combination of defects for a cumulative total of 15 or more business days during that warranty term or the appropriate time period, whichever is the earlier date.

Maryland §14-1501 *et seq.*

(d) It shall be presumed that a reasonable number of attempts have been undertaken to conform a

motor vehicle to the applicable warranties if:

(1) The same nonconformity, defect, or condition has been subject to repair 4 or more times by the manufacturer or factory branch, or its agents or authorized dealers, within the warranty period but such nonconformity, defect, or condition continues to exist; [or]

(2) The vehicle is out of service by reason of repair of 1 or more nonconformities, defects, or conditions for a cumulative total of 30 or more days during the warranty period; or,

(3) A nonconformity, defect, or condition resulting in failure of the braking or steering system has been subject to the same repair at least once within the warranty period, and the manufacturer has been notified and given the opportunity to cure the defect, and the repair does not bring the vehicle into compliance with the motor vehicle safety inspection laws of the State.

Michigan §257.1401 *et seq.*

§257.1403(3) It shall be presumed that a reasonable number of attempts have been undertaken

to repair any defect or condition if 1 of the following occurs:

(a) The same defect or condition that substantially impairs the use or value of the new motor vehicle to the consumer has been subject to repair a total of 4 or more times by the manufacturer or new motor vehicle dealer and the defect or condition continues to exist. Any repair performed on the same defect made pursuant to subsection (4) shall be included in calculating the number of repairs under this section. The consumer or his or her representative, prior to availing himself or herself of a remedy provided under subsection (1), and any time after the third attempt to repair the same defect or condition, shall give written notification, by return receipt service, to the manufacturer of the need for repair of the defect or condition in order to allow the manufacturer an opportunity to cure the defect or condition. The manufacturer shall notify the consumer as soon as reasonably possible of a reasonably accessible repair facility. After delivery of the vehicle to the designated repair facility, the manufacturer shall have 5 business days to repair the defect or condition. [or]

(b) The new motor vehicle is out of service because of repairs for a total of 30 or more days or parts of days during the term of the manufacturer's express warranty, or within 1 year from the date of delivery to the original consumer, whichever is earlier. It shall be the responsibility of the consumer, or his or her representative, prior to availing himself or herself of a remedy provided under subsection (1), and after the vehicle has been out of service for at least 25 days in a repair facility, to give written notification by return receipt service to the manufacturer of the need for repair of the defect or condition in order to allow the manufacturer an opportunity to cure the defect or condition. The manufacturer shall notify the consumer as soon as reasonably possible of a reasonably accessible repair facility. After delivery of the vehicle to the designated repair facility, the manufacturer shall have 5 business days to repair the defect or condition.

Minnesota §325F.665 *et seq.*

(b) It is presumed that a reasonable number of attempts have been undertaken to conform a new motor vehicle to the applicable express warranties, if

(1) the same nonconformity has been subject to repair four or more times by the manufacturer, its agents, or its authorized dealers within the applicable express warranty term or during the period of two years following the date of original delivery of the new motor vehicle to a consumer, whichever is the earlier date, but the nonconformity continues to exist, or,

(2) the vehicle is out of service by reason of repair for a cumulative total of 30 or more business days during the term or during the period, whichever is the earlier date.

(c) If the nonconformity results in a complete failure of the braking or steering system of the new motor vehicle and is likely to cause death or serious bodily injury if the vehicle is driven, it is presumed that a reasonable number of attempts have been undertaken to conform the vehicle to the applicable express warranties if the nonconformity has been subject to repair at least once by the manufacturer, its agents, or its authorized dealers within the applicable express warranty term or during the period of two years following the date of original delivery of the new motor vehicle to a consumer, whichever is the earlier date, and the nonconformity continues to exist.

Mississippi §63-17-151 *et seq.*

SEC. 63-17-157 For the purposes of Sections 63-17-151 *et seq.*, if a new motor vehicle does not conform to all applicable express warranties, and the consumer reports the nonconformity to the manufacturer or its agent during the term of such express warranties or during the period of one (1) year following the date of original delivery of the motor vehicle to the consumer, whichever period expires earlier, the manufacturer or its agent shall make such repairs as are necessary to conform the vehicle to such express warranties, notwithstanding the fact that such repairs are made after the expiration of such term or such one-year period.

(1) If the manufacturer or its agent cannot conform the motor vehicle to any applicable express warranty by repairing or correcting any default or condition which impairs the use, market value, or safety of the motor vehicle to the consumer after a reasonable number of attempts, the manufacturer shall give the consumer the option of having the manufacturer either replace the motor vehicle with a comparable motor vehicle acceptable to the consumer, or take title of the vehicle from the consumer and refund to the consumer the full purchase price, including all reasonably incurred collateral charges, less a reasonable allowance for the consumer's use of the vehicle. The subtraction of a reasonable allowance for use shall apply when either a replacement or refund of the motor vehicle occurs. A reasonable allowance for use shall be that sum of money arrived at by multiplying the number of miles the motor vehicle has been driven by the consumer by Twenty Cents (20cents) per mile. Refunds shall be made to the consumer and lien holder of record, if any, as their interests may appear.

Missouri Title 26, §407.560 *et seq.*

§407.571 It shall be presumed that a reasonable number of attempts have been undertaken to conform a new motor vehicle to the applicable express warranties if within the terms, conditions, or limitations of the express warranty, or during the period of one year following the date of original delivery of the new motor vehicle to a consumer, whichever expires earlier, either:

(1) The same nonconformity has been subject to repair four or more times by the manufacturer, or its agents, and such nonconformity continues to exist; or,

(2) The new vehicle is out of service by reason of repair of the nonconformity by the manufacturer, through its authorized dealer or its agents, for a cumulative total of thirty or more working days, exclusive of down time for routine maintenance as prescribed by the manufacturer, since delivery of the new vehicle to the consumer. The thirty-day period may be extended by a period of time during which repair services are not available to the consumer because of conditions beyond the control of the manufacturer or its agents.

Montana §61-4-501 *et seq.*

§61-4-504 A reasonable number of attempts to conform a new motor vehicle to the applicable express warranties is presumed to have been made if:

(1) the same nonconformity has been subject to repair four or more times by the manufacturer or its agent or authorized dealer during the warranty period but the nonconformity continues to exist; or,

(2) the vehicle is out of service because of nonconformity for a cumulative total of 30 or more business days during the warranty period after notification of the manufacturer, agent, or dealer.

Nebraska §60-2701 *et seq.*

§60-2704 It shall be presumed that a reasonable number of attempts have been undertaken to conform a motor vehicle to the applicable express warranties, if:

(1) the same nonconformity has been subject to repair four or more times by the manufacturer, its agents, or authorized dealers within the express warranty term or during the period of one year following the date of original delivery of the motor vehicle to a consumer, whichever is the earlier date, but such nonconformity continues to exist or,

(2) the vehicle is out of service by reason of repair for a cumulative total of forty or more days during such term or during such period, whichever is the earlier date.

Nevada §597.630 *et seq.*

§597.630(2) It is presumed that a reasonable number of attempts have been undertaken to conform a motor vehicle to the applicable express warranties where:

(a) The same nonconformity has been subject to repair four or more times by the manufacturer, or its agent or authorized dealer within the time the express warranty is in effect or within 1 year following the date the motor vehicle is delivered to the original buyer, whichever occurs earlier, but the nonconformity continues to exist; or.

(b) The motor vehicle is out of service for repairs for a cumulative total of 30 or more calendar days within the time the express warranty is in effect or within 1 year following the date the motor vehicle is delivered to the original buyer, whichever occurs earlier, except that if the necessary repairs cannot be made for reasons which are beyond the control of the manufacturer or its agent or authorized dealer, the number of days required to give rise to the presumption must be appropriately extended.

New Hampshire §31-357D.1 *et seq.*

§31-357D.3 VII. It shall be presumed that a reasonable number of attempts have been undertaken
to conform a motor vehicle to the applicable warranties if:

(a) The same nonconformity as identified in any written examination or repair order has been subject to repair at least 3 times by the manufacturer, its agent, or authorized dealer within the express warranty term and the same nonconformity continues to exist; or,

(b) The vehicle is out of service by reason of repair of one or more nonconformities, defects, or conditions for a cumulative total of 30 or more business days during the term of the express warranty. The term of any warranty and the 30-day period shall be extended by any period of time during which repair services were not available to the consumer because of war, invasion, strike, fire, flood, or other natural disaster. If an extension of time is necessitated due to these conditions, the manufacturer shall provide for the free use of a vehicle to the consumer whose vehicle is out of service. A vehicle shall not be deemed out of service if it is available to the consumer for a major part of the day.

New Jersey §56:12-29 *et seq.*

§56:12-33(a) It is presumed that a manufacturer or its dealer is unable to repair or correct a nonconformity within a reasonable time if, within the first 18,000 miles of operation or during the period of two years following the date of original delivery of the motor vehicle to a consumer, whichever is the earlier date:

(1) Substantially the same nonconformity has been subject to repair three or more times by the manufacturer or its dealer and the nonconformity continues to exist; or,

(2) The motor vehicle is out of service by reason of repair for one or more nonconformities for a cumulative total of 20 or more calendar days since the original delivery of the motor vehicle and a nonconformity continues to exist.

New Mexico §57-16A-1 *et seq.*

57-16A-3(C) It shall be presumed that a reasonable number of attempts as mentioned in Subsection B of this section have been undertaken to conform a new motor vehicle to the applicable express warranties if:

(1) the same uncorrected nonconformity has been subject to repair four or more times by the manufacturer or its agents or authorized dealers within the express warranty term or during the period of one year following the date of original delivery of the motor vehicle to a consumer, whichever is the earlier date, but the nonconformity continues to exist; or,

(2) the vehicle is in the possession of the manufacturer, its agent or authorized dealer for repair a cumulative total of thirty or more business days during such term or during such period whichever is the earlier date, exclusive of down time for routine maintenance as prescribed by the manufacturer.

New York §198-a *et seq.*

§198(d) It shall be presumed that a reasonable number of attempts have been undertaken to conform a motor vehicle to the applicable express warranties, if:

(1) the same nonconformity, defect or condition has been subject to repair four or more times by the manufacturer or its agents or authorized dealers within the first eighteen thousand miles of operation or during the period of two years following the date of original delivery of the motor vehicle to a consumer, whichever is the earlier date, but such nonconformity, defect or condition continues to exist: or,

(2) the vehicle is out of service by reason of repair of one or more nonconformities, defects or conditions for a cumulative total of thirty or more calendar days during either period, whichever is the earlier date.

North Carolina Article 15A, §20-351 *et seq.*

§ 20-351.5(a) It is presumed that a reasonable number of attempts have been undertaken to conform a motor vehicle to the applicable express warranties if:

(1) The same nonconformity has been presented for repair to the manufacturer, its agent, or its authorized dealer four or more times but the same nonconformity continues to exist; or,

(2) The vehicle was out of service to the consumer during or while awaiting repair of the nonconformity or a series of nonconformities for a cumulative total of 20 or more business days during any 12-month period of the warranty, provided that the consumer has notified the manufacturer directly in writing of the existence of the nonconformity or series of nonconformities and allowed the manufacturer a reasonable period, not to exceed 15 calendar days, in which to correct the nonconformity or series of nonconformities.

North Dakota §51-07-16 *et seq.*

51-07-19(1) It is presumed that a reasonable number of attempts have been undertaken to make a passenger motor vehicle conform to the applicable express warranties, if:

(a) The same nonconformity has continued to exist, despite having been subject to repair more than three times by the manufacturer, its agent, or its authorized dealer, within the express warranty term or within one year of the date of original delivery of the passenger motor vehicle to a consumer, whichever is the earlier date.

(b) The passenger motor vehicle is out of service for repair for a cumulative total of at least thirty business days during the warranty term or in a year, whichever is less.

Ohio §1345.71 *et seq.*

§1345.73 It shall be presumed that a reasonable number of attempts have been undertaken by the manufacturer, its dealer, or its authorized agent to conform a motor vehicle to any applicable express warranty if, during the period of one year following the date of original delivery or during the first eighteen thousand miles of operation, whichever is earlier, any of the following apply:

(A) Substantially the same nonconformity has been subject to repair three or more times and continues to exist; [or]

(B) The vehicle is out of service by reason of repair for a cumulative total of thirty or more calendar days; [or]

(C) There have been eight or more attempts to repair any nonconformity that substantially impairs the use and value of the motor vehicle to the consumer; [or]

(D) There has been at least one attempt to repair a nonconformity that results in a condition that is likely to cause death or serious bodily injury if the vehicle is driven, and the nonconformity continues to exist.

Oklahoma §15-901 *et seq.*

§15-901 D. It shall be presumed that a reasonable number of attempts have been undertaken to conform a motor vehicle to the applicable express warranties, if:

(1) the same nonconformity has been subject to repair four or more times by the manufacturer or its agents or authorized dealers within the express warranty term or during the period of one (1) year following the date of original delivery of the motor vehicle to a consumer, whichever is the
earlier date, but such nonconformity continues to exist or,

(2) the vehicle is out of service by reason of repair for a cumulative total of forty five (45) or more calendar days during such term or during such period, whichever is the earlier date. The term of an express warranty, such one-year period and such forty five day period shall be extended by any period of time during which repair services are not available to the consumer because of a war, invasion, strike or fire, flood or other natural disaster.

Oregon §646.315 *et seq.*

§646.345(1) It shall be presumed that a reasonable number of attempts have been undertaken to conform a motor vehicle to the applicable manufacturer's express warranties if, during the period of one year following the date of original delivery of the motor vehicle to a consumer or during the period ending on the date on which the mileage on the motor vehicle reaches 12,000 miles, whichever period ends earlier:

(a) The same nonconformity has been subject to repair or correction four or more times by the manufacturer or its agent or authorized dealer, but such nonconformity continues to exist; or,

(b) The vehicle is out of service by reason of repair or correction for a cumulative total of 30 or more business days.

Pennsylvania Title 73, Chapter 28, §1951 *et seq.*

§1956 It shall be presumed that a reasonable number of attempts have been undertaken to repair or correct a nonconformity if:

(1) The same nonconformity has been subject to repair three times by the manufacturer,

its agents or authorized dealers and the nonconformity still exists; or,

(2) The vehicle is out-of-service by reason of any nonconformity for a cumulative total of

30 or more calendar days.

Rhode Island §31-5.2-1 *et seq.*

§31-5.2-5(a) A reasonable number of attempts shall be presumed to have been undertaken to conform a motor vehicle to any applicable express or implied warranties if:

(1) the same nonconformity has been subject to repair four (4) or more times by the manufacturer or its agents or authorized dealers or lessors within the term of protection, but the nonconformity continues to exist or the nonconformity has recurred within the term of protection, or,

(2) the vehicle is out of service by reason of the repair of any nonconformity for a cumulative total of thirty (30) or more calendar days during the term of protection; provided, however, the manufacturer shall be afforded one additional opportunity, not to exceed seven (7) calendar days, to cure any nonconformity arising during the term of protection, notwithstanding the fact that the additional opportunity to cure commences after the term of protection.

South Carolina §56-28-10 *et seq.*

56-28-50(A) It is presumed that a reasonable number of attempts have been undertaken to conform a motor vehicle to the applicable express warranties if:

(1) the same nonconformity has been subject to repair three or more times by the manufacturer, or its agent, within the express warranty term, but the nonconformity continues to exist; or,

(2) the vehicle is out of service by reason of repair for a cumulative total of thirty or more calendar days during the express warranty.

South Dakota §32-6D-1 *et seq.*

32-6D-5 It is presumed that reasonable attempts to correct a nonconforming condition have been allowed by the consumer if, during the period of twenty-four months following delivery of the vehicle or twenty-four thousand miles, whichever first occurs, either of the following events occurred:

(1) The same nonconforming condition was subject to repair attempts four or more times by the manufacturer, or its authorized dealers, at least one of which occurred during the lemon law rights period, plus a final attempt by the manufacturer, and the same nonconforming condition continues to exist; or,

(2) The motor vehicle was out of service and in the custody of the manufacturer or an authorized dealer due to repair attempts including the final repair attempt, one of which occurred during the lemon law rights period, for a cumulative

total of thirty calendar days, unless the repair could not be performed because of conditions beyond the control of the manufacturer or authorized dealers, such as war, invasion, strike, fire, flood, or other natural disaster.

Tennessee §55-24-201 *et seq.*

55-24-205(a) It shall be presumed that a reasonable number of attempts have been undertaken to conform a motor vehicle to the applicable express warranties, if:

(1) The same nonconformity has been subject to repair four (4) or more times by the manufacturer or its agents or authorized dealers, but such nonconformity continues to exist; or,

(2) The vehicle is out of service by reason of repair for a cumulative total of thirty (30) or more calendar days during the term of protection.

Texas §4413(36)3.08(i) *et seq.*

§4413(36)3.08(i)(d) There is a rebuttable presumption that a reasonable number of attempts have been undertaken to conform a motor vehicle to the applicable express warranties if:

(1) the same nonconformity has been subject to repair four or more times by the manufacturer, converter, or distributor, its agent, or its franchised dealer and two of the repair attempts have been made within a period of 12 months following the date of original delivery to an owner, or 12,000 miles, whichever occurs first, and the other two repair attempts occur within the 12 months or 12,000 miles immediately following the date of the second repair attempt, whichever occurs first, but such nonconformity continues to exist; [or]

(2) the same nonconformity creates a serious safety hazard and has caused the vehicle to have been subject to repair two or more times by the manufacturer, converter, or distributor, or an authorized agent or franchised dealer, and at least one attempt to repair the nonconformity was made in the period of 12 months or 12,000 miles, whichever occurs first, and at least one other attempt made in the period of 12 months or 12,000 miles after the first repair attempt, whichever occurs first, but the nonconformity continues to exist; or,

(3) the vehicle is out of service for repair for a cumulative total of 30 or more days in the 24 months or 24,000 miles, whichever occurs first, and at least two repair attempts were made in the first 12 months or 12,000 miles immediately following the date of original delivery to an owner and a nonconformity still exists that substantially impairs the vehicle's use or market value.

Utah §13-20-1 *et seq.*

13-20-5(1) It is presumed that a reasonable number of attempts have been undertaken to conform a motor vehicle to the applicable express warranties, if:

(a) the same nonconformity has been subject to repair four or more times by the manufacturer, its agent, or its authorized dealer within the express warranty term or during the one-year period following the date of original delivery of the motor vehicle to a consumer, whichever is earlier, but the nonconformity continues to exist; or,

(b) the vehicle is out of service to the consumer because of repair for a cumulative total of 30 or more business days during the warranty term or during the one-year period, whichever is earlier.

Vermont Title 9, Chapter 115, §4170 *et seq.*

Chapter 115, §4170(g) It shall be presumed that a reasonable number of attempts have been undertaken to conform a motor vehicle to the applicable warranties if:

(1) the same nonconformity as identified in any written examination or repair order has been subject to repair at least three times by the manufacturer, its agent or authorized dealer and at least the first repair attempt occurs within the express warranty term and the same nonconformity continues to exist, or,

(2) the vehicle is out of service by reason of repair of one or more nonconformities, defects or conditions for a cumulative total of 30 or more calendar days during the term of the express warranty. **** A vehicle shall not be deemed out of service if it is available to the consumer for a major part of the day.

Virginia §59.1-207.9 *et seq.*

§59.1-207.9B It shall be presumed that a reasonable number of attempts have been undertaken to conform a motor vehicle to any warranty and that the motor vehicle is significantly impaired if during the period of eighteen months following the date of original delivery of the motor vehicle to the consumer either:

(1) The same nonconformity has been subject to repair three or more times by the manufacturer, its agents or its authorized dealers and the same nonconformity continues to exist; [or]

(2) The nonconformity is a serious safety defect and has been subject to repair one or more times by the manufacturer, its agent or its authorized dealer and the same nonconformity continues to exist; or,

(3) The motor vehicle is out of service due to repair for a cumulative total of thirty calendar days, unless such repairs could not be performed because of conditions beyond the control of the manufacturer, its agents or authorized dealers, including war, invasion, strike, fire, flood or other natural disasters.

Washington §19.118.005 *et seq.*

§19.118.005(2) Reasonable number of attempts, except in the case of a new motor vehicle that is a motor home acquired after June 30, 1998, shall be deemed to have been undertaken by the manufacturer, its agent, or the new motor vehicle dealer to conform the new motor vehicle to the warranty within the warranty period, if:

(a) The same serious safety defect has been subject to diagnosis or repair two or more times, at least one of which is during the period of coverage of the applicable manufacturer's written warranty, and the serious safety defect continues to exist; [or]

(b) the same nonconformity has been subject to diagnosis or repair four or more times, at least one of which is during the period of coverage of the applicable manufacturer's written warranty, and the nonconformity continues to exist; or,

(c) the vehicle is out of service by reason of diagnosis or repair of one or more nonconformities for a cumulative total of thirty calendar days, at least fifteen of them during the period of the applicable manufacturer's written warranty. For purposes of this subsection, the manufacturer's written warranty shall be at least one year after the date of the original delivery to the consumer of the vehicle or the first twelve thousand miles of operation, whichever occurs first.

West Virginia §46A-6A-1 *et seq.*

§46A-6A-5(a) It is presumed that a reasonable number of attempts have been undertaken to conform a new motor vehicle to the applicable express warranties, if the same nonconformity has been subject to repair three or more times by the manufacturer, its gents or its authorized dealers within the express warranty term or during the period of one year following the date of original delivery of the motor vehicle to the consumer, whichever is the earlier date, and the nonconformity continues to exist, or the vehicle is out of service by reason of repair for a cumulative total of thirty or more calendar days during the term or during the one-year period, whichever is the earlier date.

(b) If the nonconformity results in a condition which is likely to cause death or serious bodily injury if the vehicle is driven, it is presumed that a reasonable number of attempts have been undertaken to conform the vehicle to the applicable express warranties if the nonconformity has been subject to repair at least once by the manufacturer within the express warranty term or during the period of one year following the date of original delivery of the motor vehicle to a consumer, whichever is the earlier date, and the nonconformity continues to exist.

Wisconsin §218.015 *et seq.*

§218.015(h) "Reasonable attempt to repair" means any of the following occurring within the term of an express warranty applicable to a new motor vehicle or within one year after first delivery of the motor vehicle to a consumer, whichever is sooner:

(1) The same nonconformity with the warranty is subject to repair by the manufacturer, motor vehicle lessor or any of the manufacturer's authorized motor vehicle dealers at least 4 times and the nonconformity continues. [or]

(2) The motor vehicle is out of service for an aggregate of at least 30 days because of warranty nonconformities.

Wyoming §40-17-101 *et seq.*

§40-17-101(d) It is presumed that a reasonable number of attempts have been undertaken to conform a motor vehicle to express warranty if within one (1) year following the original delivery of the motor vehicle to the consumer, whichever is later:

(i) The same nonconformity has been subject to repair more than three (3) times by the manufacturer, its agents or its authorized dealers and the same nonconformity continues to exist; or,

(ii) The vehicle is out of service due to repair for a cumulative total of thirty (30) business days.

Appendix D
The Magnuson-Moss Warranty—Federal Trade Commission Improvement Act

The Magnuson-Moss Warranty Act is also known as the Federal Lemon Law. Its official citation is 15 USC §2301, and the important thing to remember is that it applies everywhere in the United States, and covers all warranted consume goods costing more than $25. Like any other Federal Statute, its full text runs many pages in length, and there are volumes of case law from each state interpreting it. However, some of the more important sections are excerpted below.

§2301. Definitions
For the purposes of this chapter:

(1) The term "consumer product" means any tangible personal property which is distributed in commerce and which is normally used for personal, family, or household purposes (including any such property intended to be attached to or installed in any real property without regard to whether it is so attached or installed).

(2) The term "Commission" means the Federal Trade Commission.

(3) The term "consumer" means a buyer (other than for purposes of resale) of any consumer product, any person to whom such product is transferred during the duration of an implied or written warranty (or service contract) applicable to the product, and any other person who is entitled by the terms of such warranty (or service contract) or under applicable State law to enforce against the warrantor (or service contractor) the obligations of the warranty (or service contract).

(4) The term "supplier" means any person engaged in the business of making a consumer product directly or indirectly available to consumers.

(5) The term "warrantor" means any supplier or other person who gives or offers to give a written warranty or who is or may be obligated under an implied warranty.

(6) The term "written warranty" means -

> (A) any written affirmation of fact or written promise made in connection with the sale of a consumer product by a supplier to a buyer which relates to the nature of the material or workmanship and affirms or promises that such material or workmanship is defect free or will meet a specified level of performance over a specified period of time, or

> (B) any undertaking in writing in connection with the sale by a supplier of a consumer product to refund, repair, replace, or take other remedial action with respect to such product in the event that such product fails to meet the specifications set forth in the undertaking, which written affirmation, promise, or undertaking becomes part of the basis of the bargain between a supplier and a buyer for purposes other than resale of such product.

(7) The term "implied warranty" means an implied warranty arising under State law (as modified by sections 2308 and 2304(a) of this title) in connection with the sale by a supplier of a consumer product.

(8) The term "service contract" means a contract in writing to perform, over a fixed period of time or for a specified duration, services relating to the maintenance or repair (or both) of a consumer product.

(9) The term "reasonable and necessary maintenance" consists of those operations

> (A) which the consumer reasonably can be expected to perform or have performed and

> (B) which are necessary to keep any consumer product performing its intended function and operating at a reasonable level of performance.

(10) The term "remedy" means whichever of the following actions the warrantor elects:

> (A) repair,

> (B) replacement, or

> (C) refund; except that the warrantor may not elect refund unless

(i)the warrantor is unable to provide replacement and repair is not commercially practicable or cannot be timely made, or
(ii) the consumer is willing to accept such refund.

(11) The term "replacement" means furnishing a new consumer product which is identical or reasonably equivalent to the warranted consumer product.

(12) The term "refund" means refunding the actual purchase price (less reasonable depreciation based on actual use where permitted by rules of the Commission).

(13) The term "distributed in commerce" means sold in commerce, introduced or delivered for introduction into commerce, or held for sale or distribution after introduction into commerce.

(14) The term "commerce" means trade, traffic, commerce, or transportation -
(A) between a place in a State and any place outside thereof, or
(B) which affects trade, traffic, commerce, or transportation described in subparagraph (A).

(15) The term "State" means a State, the District of Columbia, the Commonwealth of Puerto Rico, the Virgin Islands, Guam, the Canal Zone, or American Samoa. The term "State law" includes a law of the United States applicable only to the District of Columbia or only to a territory or possession of the United States; and the term "Federal law" excludes any State law.

§2302. Rules governing contents of warranties
(a) Full and conspicuous disclosure of terms and conditions; additional requirements for contents. In order to improve the adequacy of information available to consumers, prevent deception, and improve competition in the marketing of consumer products, any warrantor warranting a consumer product to a consumer by means of a written warranty shall, to the extent required by rules of the Commission, fully and conspicuously disclose in simple and readily understood language the terms and conditions of such warranty. Such rules may require inclusion in the written warranty of any of the following items among others:

(1) The clear identification of the names and addresses of the warrantors.

(2) The identity of the party or parties to whom the warranty is extended.

(3) The products or parts covered.

(4) A statement of what the warrantor will do in the event of a defect, malfunction, or failure to conform with such written warranty—at whose expense—and for what period of time.

(5) A statement of what the consumer must do and expenses he must bear.

(6) Exceptions and exclusions from the terms of the warranty.

(7) The step-by-step procedure which the consumer should take in order to obtain performance of any obligation under the warranty, including the identification of any person or class of persons authorized to perform the obligations set forth in the warranty.

(8) Information respecting the availability of any informal dispute settlement procedure offered by the warrantor and a recital, where the warranty so provides, that the purchaser may be required to resort to such procedure before pursuing any legal remedies in the courts.

(9) A brief, general description of the legal remedies available to the consumer.

(10) The time at which the warrantor will perform any obligations under the warranty.

(11) The period of time within which, after notice of a defect, malfunction, or failure to conform with the warranty, the warrantor will perform any obligations under the warranty.

(12) The characteristics or properties of the products, or parts thereof, that are not covered by the warranty.

(13) The elements of the warranty in words or phrases which would not mislead a reasonable, average consumer as to the nature or scope of the warranty.

(b) Availability of terms to consumer; manner and form for presentation and display of information; duration; extension of period for written warranty or service contract.

1. (A) The Commission shall prescribe rules requiring that the terms of any written warranty on a consumer product be made available to the consumer (or prospective consumer) prior to the sale of the product to him.

(B) The Commission may prescribe rules for determining the manner and form in which information with respect to any written warranty of a consumer product shall be clearly and conspicuously presented or displayed so as not to mislead the reasonable, average consumer, when such information is contained in advertising, labeling, point-of-sale material, or other representations in writing.

(2) Nothing in this chapter (other than paragraph (3) of this subsection) shall be deemed to authorize the Commission to prescribe the duration of written warranties given or to require that a consumer product or any of its components be warranted.

(3) The Commission may prescribe rules for extending the period of time a written warranty or service contract is in effect to correspond with any period of time in excess of a reasonable period (not less than 10 days) during which the consumer is deprived of the use of such consumer product by reason of failure of the product to conform with the written warranty or by reason of the failure of the warrantor (or service contractor) to carry out such warranty (or service contract) within the period specified in the warranty (or service contract).

§2303. Designation of written warranties

(a) Full (statement of duration) or limited warranty. Any warrantor warranting a consumer product by means of a written warranty shall clearly and conspicuously designate such warranty in the following manner, unless exempted from doing so by the Commission pursuant to subsection (c) of this section:

(1) If the written warranty meets the Federal minimum standards for warranty set forth in section 2304 of this title, then it shall be conspicuously designated a "full (statement of duration) warranty".

(2) If the written warranty does not meet the Federal minimum standards for warranty set forth in section 2304 of this title, then it shall be conspicuously designated a "limited warranty".

§2304 Federal minimum standards for warranties

(a) Remedies under written warranty; duration of implied warranty; exclusion or limitation on consequential damages for breach of written or implied warranty; election of refund or replacement. In order for a warrantor warranting a consumer product by means of a written warranty to meet the Federal minimum standards for warranty -

(1) such warrantor must as a minimum remedy such consumer product within a reasonable time and without charge, in the case of a defect, malfunction, or failure to conform with such written warranty;

(2) notwithstanding section 2308(b) of this title, such warrantor may not impose any limitation on the duration of any implied warranty on the product;

(3) such warrantor may not exclude or limit consequential damages for breach of any written or implied warranty on such product, unless such exclusion or limitation conspicuously appears on the face of the warranty; and

(4) if the product (or a component part thereof) contains a defect or malfunction after a reasonable number of attempts by the warrantor to remedy defects or malfunctions in such product, such warrantor must permit the consumer to elect either a refund for, or replacement without charge of, such product or part (as the case may be). The Commission may by rule specify for purposes of this paragraph, what constitutes a reasonable number of attempts to remedy particular kinds of defects or malfunctions under different circumstances. If the warrantor replaces a component part of a consumer product, such replacement shall include installing the part in the product without charge.

(b) Duties and conditions imposed on consumer by warrantor

(1) In fulfilling the duties under subsection (a) of this section respecting a written warranty, the warrantor shall not impose any duty other than notification upon any consumer as a condition of securing remedy of any consumer product which malfunctions, is defective, or does not conform to the written warranty, unless the warrantor has demonstrated in a rulemaking proceeding, or can demonstrate in an administrative or judicial enforcement proceeding (including private enforcement), or in an informal dispute settlement proceeding, that such a duty is reasonable.

(2) Notwithstanding paragraph (1), a warrantor may require, as a condition to replacement of, or refund for, any consumer product under subsection (a) of this section, that such consumer product shall be made available to the warrantor free and clear of liens and other encumbrances, except as otherwise provided by rule or order of the Commission in cases in which such a requirement would not be practicable.

***

(3) The duties under subsection (a) of this section extend from the warrantor to each person who is a consumer with respect to the consumer product.

(c) Waiver of standards. The performance of the duties under subsection (a) of this section shall not be required of the warrantor if he can show that the defect, malfunction, or failure of any warranted consumer product to conform with a written warranty, was caused by damage (not resulting from defect or malfunction) while in the possession of the consumer, or unreasonable use (including failure to provide reasonable and necessary maintenance).

(d) Remedy without charge. For purposes of this section and of section 2302(c) of this title, the term "without charge" means that the warrantor may not assess the consumer for any costs the warrantor or his representatives incur in connection with the required remedy of a warranted consumer product. An obligation under subsection (a)(1)(A) of this section to remedy without charge does not necessarily require the warrantor to compensate the consumer for incidental expenses; however, if any incidental expenses are incurred because the remedy is not made within a reasonable time or because the warrantor imposed an unreasonable duty upon the consumer as a condition of securing remedy, then the consumer shall be entitled to recover reasonable incidental expenses which are so incurred in any action against the warrantor.

(e) Incorporation of standards to products designated with full warranty for purposes of judicial actions. If a supplier designates a warranty applicable to a consumer product as a "full (statement of duration)" warranty, then the warranty on such product shall, for purposes of any action under section 2310(d) of this title or under any State law, be deemed to incorporate at least the minimum requirements of this section and rules prescribed under this section.

Appendix E
The Uniform Commercial Code

The Uniform Commercial Code is a state law that exists in one form or another in every state. The UCCs of the various states were adopted, modeled from a standard created by a national conference which was convened to create a set of rules by which merchants and consumers could conduct business, knowing what their rights would be before a transaction took place. Much of what is codified by the UCC was already the law in many states; the UCC made the law more accessible by placing all of the statutes regarding many of these topics in one place. Of importance to consumers is the law of warranty, much of which is found in Article 2 of the UCC. Keep in mind that in each state, the actual statute or code reference will probably be different than the UCC numbers given here, although you can often use these numbers to locate the section you seek once you have found the UCC in your state. For instance, to find §2-313 of the UCC in Michigan, a consumer would look in the 440 section of the Michigan Compiled Laws, for MCL 440.2313.

Also remember that each state has the right to change or modify statutes that it adopts. The UCC in your state may read differently, or even be numbered differently than the selected sections below. Always consult with a local attorney before relying on any statute, regardless of the source.

§2-313. Express warranty; creation by affirmation, promise, description, sample; affirmation of value

§2-313. (1) Express warranties by the seller are created as follows:

1. Any affirmation of fact or promise made by the seller to the buyer which relates to the goods and becomes part of the basis of the bargain creates an express warranty that the goods shall conform to the affirmation or promise.

(b) Any description of the goods which is made part of the basis of the bargain creates an express warranty that the goods shall conform to the description.

(c) Any sample or model which is made part of the basis of the bargain creates an express warranty that the whole of the goods shall conform to the sample or model.

(2) It is not necessary to the creation of an express warranty that the seller use formal words such as "warrant" or "guarantee" or that he or she have a specific intention to make a warranty, but an affirmation merely of the value of the goods or a statement purporting to be merely the seller's opinion or commendation of the goods does not create a warranty.

§2-314 Implied warranty; merchantability, course of dealing, usage of trade

§2-314. (1) Unless excluded or modified, a warranty that the goods shall be merchantable is implied in a contract for their sale if the seller is a merchant with respect to goods of that kind. Under this section the serving for value of food or drink to be consumed either on the premises or elsewhere is a sale.

(2) Goods to be merchantable must be at least such as

    (a) pass without objection in the trade under the contract description; and

    (b) in the case of fungible goods, are of fair average quality within the description; and

    (c) are fit for the ordinary purposes for which such goods are used; and

    (d) run, within the variations permitted by the agreement, of even kind, quality and quantity within each unit and among all units involved; and

    (e) are adequately contained, packaged, and labeled as the agreement may require; and

    (f) conform to the promises or affirmations of fact made on the container or label if any.

(3) Unless excluded or modified, other implied warranties may arise from course of dealing or usage of trade.

§2-315. Implied warranty; fitness for particular purpose

§2-315. Where the seller at the time of contracting has reason to know any particular purpose for which the goods are required and that the buyer is relying on the seller's skill or judgment to select or furnish suitable goods, there is unless excluded or modified under the next section an implied warranty that the goods shall be fit for such purpose.

§2-316. Exclusion or modification of warranties

§2-316. (1) Words or conduct relevant to the creation of an express warranty and words or conduct tending to negate or limit warranty shall be construed wherever reasonable as consistent with each other; but subject to the provisions of this article on parol or extrinsic evidence (section 2-202) negation or limitation is inoperative to the extent that such construction is unreasonable.

(2) Subject to subsection (3), to exclude or modify the implied warranty of merchantability or any part of it the language must mention merchantability and in case of a writing must be conspicuous, and to exclude or modify any implied warranty of fitness the exclusion must be by a writing and conspicuous. Language to exclude all implied warranties of fitness is sufficient if it states, for example, that "There are no warranties which extend beyond the description on the face hereof."

(3) Notwithstanding subsection (2):

> (a) unless the circumstances indicate otherwise, all implied warranties are excluded by expressions like "as is", "with all faults" or other language which in common understanding calls the buyer's attention to the exclusion of warranties and makes plain that there is no implied warranty; and

> (b) when the buyer before entering into the contract has examined the goods or the sample or model as fully as he desired or has refused to examine the goods there is no implied warranty with regard to defects which an examination ought in the circumstances to have revealed to him; and

> (c) an implied warranty can also be excluded or modified by course of dealing or course of performance or usage of trade; and

> (d) with respect to the sale of cattle, hogs, or sheep, there is no implied warranty that the cattle, hogs, or sheep are free from disease, if the seller shows that all state and federal law concerning animal health has been satisfied.

(4) Remedies for breach of warranty can be limited in accordance with the provisions of this article on liquidation or limitation of damages and on contractual modification of remedy (§§2-718 and 2-719).

§2-317. Cumulation and conflict of warranties express or implied

§2-317. Warranties whether express or implied shall be construed as consistent with each other and as cumulative, but if such construction is unreasonable the intention of the parties shall determine which warranty is dominant. In ascertaining that intention the following rules apply:

(a) Exact or technical specifications displace an inconsistent sample or model or general language of description.

(b) A sample from an existing bulk displaces inconsistent general language of description.

(c) Express warranties displace inconsistent implied warranties other than an implied warranty of fitness for a particular purpose.

§2-608. Acceptance of goods; revocation, time, notice, effect

§2-608. (1) The buyer may revoke his acceptance of a lot or commercial unit whose nonconformity substantially impairs its value to him if he has accepted it

> (a) on the reasonable assumption that its nonconformity would be cured and it has not been seasonably cured; or

> (b) without discovery of such nonconformity if his acceptance was reasonably induced either by the difficulty of discovery before acceptance or by the seller's assurances.

(2) Revocation of acceptance must occur within a reasonable time after the buyer discovers or should have discovered the ground for it and before any substantial change in condition of the goods which is not caused by their own defects. It is not effective until the buyer notifies the seller of it.

(3) A buyer who so revokes has the same rights and duties with regard to the goods involved as if he had rejected them.

§2-711. Nondelivery, repudiation, rejection or revocation of acceptance; buyer's remedies; security interest in goods

§2-711. (1) Where the seller fails to make delivery or repudiates or the buyer rightfully rejects or justifiably revokes acceptance then with respect to any goods involved, and with respect to the whole if the breach goes to the whole contract (§2-612), the buyer may cancel and whether or not he has done so may in addition to recovering so much of the price as has been paid

> (a) "cover" and have damages under the next section as to all the goods affected whether or not they have been identified to the contract; or

> (b) recover damages for nondelivery as provided in this article (§2-713).

(2) Where the seller fails to deliver or repudiates the buyer may also

> (a) if the goods have been identified recover them as provided in this article; or

> (b) in a proper case obtain specific performance or replevy or recover the goods as provided in this article (§2-716).

(3) On rightful rejection or justifiable revocation of acceptance a buyer has a security interest in goods in his possession or control for any payments made on their price and any expenses reasonably incurred in their inspection, receipt, transportation, care and custody and may hold such goods and resell them in like manner as an aggrieved seller (§2-706).

Glossary of Commonly Used Terms in the Consumer Law Field

Certificate of Origin: The birth certificate for the automobile, showing the manufacturer as the original "owner" of the auto, along with its place of manufacture, VIN, and so on.

CNV: Abbreviation for Can/Could Not Verify used by service technicians who claim to not be able to verify the consumer's complaints.

Deficiency: The amount of money still owed on a loan or lease after the lender has sold the vehicle at auction for less than is owed on the loan. The opposite situation creates a surplus, where the vehicle sells for more than is owed on the loan.

NHTSA: National Highway Transportation Safety Administration. A division of the Department of Transportation that oversees the safety of automobiles, including the issuing of recalls and cataloguing of consumer complaints. They have a very helpful website at

NPF: Abbreviation for No Problem Found used by service technicians who claim to not be able to verify the consumer's complaints.

Payoff: The cost of paying off a loan at a given time, usually early. This amount is usually less than merely adding up the remaining payments since it eliminates the payment of interest that has not been incurred yet.

Recalls: the official action taken by a manufacturer regarding a known safety problem. These are sent to consumers directly telling them what the problem is and how and where they can have it fixed at no charge. Recalls information is also tracked by NHTSA at

Repair Order, "RO": The paper that is written up when a consumer brings a vehicle in for repairs under the manufacturer's warranty. This document is very important in that it helps a consumer prove the elements of the lemon law claim by showing what complaints were addressed when, and how long the vehicle was in for repair.

Title History: The records of ownership with respect to a vehicle from its manufacture to present day. The title history of a brand new car only includes the Certificate of Origin. An older model's history may run into dozens, if not more, owners.

TSB: Technical Service Bulletins are issued by the manufacturers when a problem occurs in many automobiles, suggesting that the problem is widespread. The TSB usually describes the symptoms and proposes a repair, and although they are written for the dealerships, they are available from several sources, including from

UDTPA, UDAP: Unfair and Deceptive Trade Practices Act, Unfair and Deceptive Acts and Practices. Two model statutes which many states used to write their own consumer laws. Most have a laundry list of things which are unlawful in a consumer setting and allow for the recovery of damages as well as attorney's fees and court costs. Some contain punitive provisions. Some also empower state agencies to take action against merchants who violate their acts.

Uniform Commercial Code ("U.C.C."): The set of laws and rules governing commercial transactions which have been adopted in all states. They do vary slightly from state to state however, even though most states adopted their UCCs from the same model. It is the UCC which spells out warranty rights and laws, as well as a consumer's right to revoke acceptance. Article 9 of the UCC also defines the rights and remedies of the parties in a purchase money security interest—the lending of money to purchase an item which is used as collateral on the underlying loan—such as an auto loan.

VIN: Abbreviation for Vehicle Identification Number. Each automobile has one, unique to itself, by which it is identified on its title. In cars and trucks the number is found several places, but most prominently on a metal tag visible by standing next to the driver's door and look straight down through the window at the back edge of the dashboard.

www.ingramcontent.com/pod-product-compliance
Lightning Source LLC
Chambersburg PA
CBHW051340170526
45166CB00002B/899